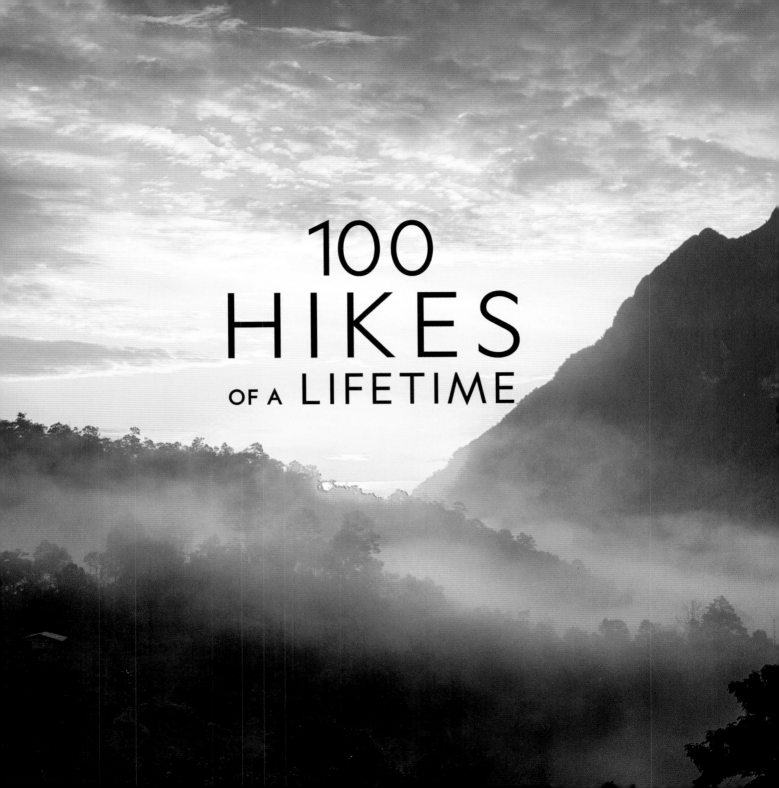

100
HIKES
of a LIFETIME

100 HIKES OF A LIFETIME

The World's Ultimate Scenic Trails

KATE SIBER

FOREWORD BY ANDREW SKURKA

NATIONAL GEOGRAPHIC

WASHINGTON, D.C.

CONTENTS

PAGE 1: Hike to the top of Doi Luang Chiang Dao, a popular northern Thailand spot to watch the sunrise (page 350).

PAGES 2-3: The Rapa River Delta cuts through Sarek National Park (page 202) and can be seen from the summit of many hiking trails.

LEFT: A barren forest of 1,000-year-old sun-scorched trees dots the Sossusvlei dunes in Namibia (page 250).

FOREWORD

Nearly 20 years ago I went backpacking for the first time on an overnight in Yosemite National Park. It was a disaster. I inched up the trail, shouldering a 50-pound (23-kg) pack, loaded with unnecessary items—many that even went unused. I didn't sleep for a second, inadequately insulated from the snowpack and worried that a bear was moments away from ripping my tent apart. And I had a long, thirsty hike out the next morning, since my water bottle had frozen solid.

Thankfully, Yosemite—home to famous landmarks like Nevada Falls and El Capitan—is distractingly magnificent. So beautiful that I decided my overnight trip was enjoyable enough to try another one. A big one, actually: Two months later I pulled up to Springer Mountain in Georgia, the southern terminus of the Appalachian Trail, with the intention of walking 2,175 miles (3,500 km) to Maine.

Backpacking need not be hard. Excellent books, websites, videos, and courses can teach you how to do it the right way. Regrettably, I decided to learn through trial and error. The Appalachian Trail was not the three-month communion with nature I'd anticipated, but rather the most difficult undertaking of my life, especially during those early miles. I had no solutions for subfreezing nighttime temperatures, ceaseless rainfall, biting insects, high humidity, or tortured feet; and I struggled with overuse injuries, loneliness, and self-doubt.

But what the trail failed to give me in Thoreau-like insights about the natural world, it made up for in personal growth. When I finally stood atop Katahdin—not the result of conquering so much as enduring and adapting—I

A rainbow forms in the mist of Bridalveil Fall at Yosemite National Park in California (page 36).

was more self-aware and self-sufficient, and more confident in my potential than when I'd started. At 21 years old, I'd learned that monstrous goals can be taken on literally one step at a time.

When I returned to my off-the-trail life afterward, I began to appreciate the experience even more. For one-fourth of a year, I possessed an exceptional sense of daily purpose, and had immersed myself in a single activity with no breaks or distractions. Never before had I been afforded that opportunity and simple existence.

I became a dirtbag hiker for the remainder of my 20s. Among a handful of shorter trips, I walked from the Atlantic to the Pacific in 11 months,

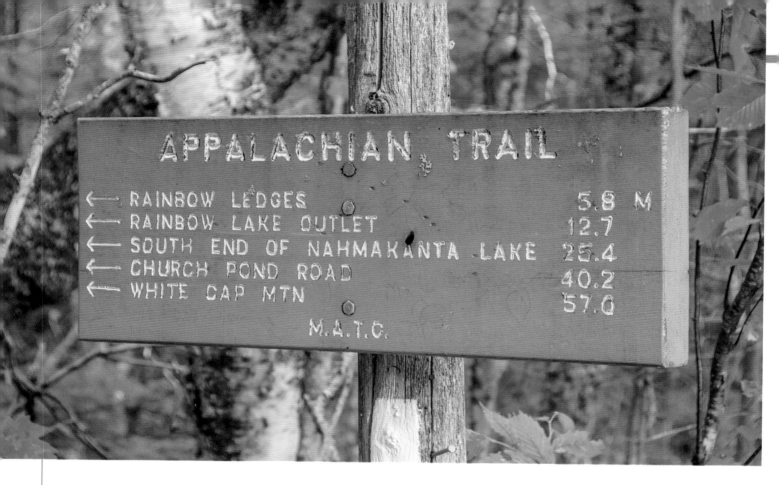

APPALACHIAN TRAIL

← RAINBOW LEDGES   5.8 M
← RAINBOW LAKE OUTLET   12.7
← SOUTH END OF NAHMAKANTA LAKE   25.4
← CHURCH POND ROAD   40.2
← WHITE CAP MTN   57.0

M.A.T.C.

circumnavigated the American West in seven months, and looped around Alaska and the Yukon in six months.

My learning curve expectedly plateaued as I racked up miles under foot and nights on the ground. I became more certain about the gear that I needed and the food that best fueled me, and I mastered the skills that made the difference between surviving and thriving: how to navigate on and off trails, care for blisters and maceration, find relatively warm and dry campsites, start fires in cold and wet conditions, protect my food from bears, manage mosquitoes, cross raging rivers, and hike across steep snowfields.

A guide post on the Appalachian Trail directs hikers to spots along the popular 2,192-mile (3,528-km) trek.

As the mechanics of backpacking became second nature, my mental slack shifted to the landscapes through which I walked. At a three-mile-an-hour (5 km/h) pace, I learned about tree species, glacial erosion, wildlife patterns, and the night sky; I saw complex political issues like Western water rights from multiple angles, including climate, history, agriculture, and urban planning; I witnessed the depopulation of agricultural areas and the brain drain from rural America; and I grappled with the romantic conception of wilderness as opposed to its intimidating reality.

By my 30th birthday I'd walked more than 30,000 miles (48,280 km), nearly all of them solo. It had been an experientially rich decade, but I was tired of the associated geographic and financial uncertainty. In unintentionally quick succession, I started a guiding service, bought a house, and fell in love.

Sharing wilderness experiences with others gave backpacking yet another new dimension. After just a long weekend together, I know most clients better than I know my neighbors. The backcountry is an intimate and distraction-free setting that brings strangers together in unique ways: scrambling up airy passes, sharing dinners of beans and rice with Fritos and cheese, helping each other secure tents in high winds, and drying out by the campfire after a daylong soaker.

This book offers 100 world-class opportunities to experience the essence of hiking and backpacking: connecting deeply with yourself, with a landscape, and with others. Included are itineraries that range from done-in-a-day jaunts to months-long adventures, suitable for those who are still learning what to pack and how to sleep soundly in bear country, as well as for those who have completely dialed in their gear, supplies, and skills. You will find desert hikes, iconic pilgrimages, forest havens, coastal wonders, and historic trails. There is something for every type of hiker and traveler. All you're left to do is flip through these pages, settle on a destination, lace up those shoes, and go!

—Andrew Skurka

INTRODUCTION

From the South Rim of the Grand Canyon, a trail snakes down cliffs deep into a labyrinth of stone. The Havasupai people have lived in a flat verdant valley here for countless generations, growing beans, corn, and squash and reaping the blessings of a limestone aquifer filled with blue-green water. Today, the area is still only reachable on foot, and hikers arrive in numbers, drawn by the legendary turquoise waterfalls that pour off cliffs and collect in idyllic pools below the village of Supai.

On a warm fall evening on my first big backpacking trip, I arrived after 10 miles (16 km) of hoofing it over sand and stone to catch my first glimpse of Havasupai Falls, a 100-foot (30-m) stunner that catapults off a travertine ledge. Smoothed by centuries of flowing water, it appears as if it is melting. Growing up in a big eastern city, I felt as if a curtain had been pulled back; all of a sudden I realized that the wonders of this Earth were so much greater than I had ever imagined. What other marvels hid in this planet's secret recesses?

Unexpected moments like these are some of the fruits of traveling the world on foot. By the power of one's own body and the grace of one's own gait, it's possible to explore new worlds with an intimacy inaccessible to those attached to speedier modes of transport. For most of our story as a species, we saw our surroundings at a pace no greater than six miles an hour (10 km/h). Reclaiming that pace offers opportunities to connect with our planet in the most satisfying of ways. This book is a testament to those possibilities.

Each hike in this volume offers a uniquely memorable experience. In the Brooks Range of Alaska, for example, walk in the footsteps of people who have survived off the arctic caribou herds for centuries. On Germany's Rheinsteig, traipse past romantic castles, ancient villages, and tidy vineyards. On the island of Pohnpei, wade through a river to immerse yourself in a parade

A cave on the west of Mount Arbel, once a hideout for Jewish rebels in 37 B.C., looks out over the Israel National Trail (page 292).

of waterfalls ensconced in jungle. And in the holy lands of the Middle East, trace the routes of biblical prophets through deserts of yore on the Israel Trail.

Enjoy a journey to every continent and to ecosystems from deserts to oceans, jungles to tundra. You'll find hikes that range from flat afternoon rambles to challenging multiweek expeditions—as well as fascinating asides about the wildlife, cultures, and histories that make each place unique.

Venturing into these wilds is not only about amassing noteworthy tales, it's about claiming our birthright. Hiking, at its best, is a means of remembering who we are and our context on this wild planet. Let these pages ignite your imagination with what's possible—then find your own moments of transcendence somewhere out there on a winding path. I'll see you there.

THE ESSENTIAL GEAR GUIDE

For multiday backpacking hikes, Andrew Skurka, author of *The Ultimate Hiker's Gear Guide,* is a pro at knowing what to pack. Here are his essentials for clothing and footwear, which can come in handy on shorter hikes, too.

CLOTHING: The Core 13

The Core 13 is Skurka's tight collection of backpacking clothing that can be mixed and matched to create applicable outfits for all variations of three-season conditions. Only on a long-distance trip through multiple environments would all 13 pieces be necessary; normally six to 10 will get the job done.

ITEM	MY PICK OR SUGGESTION	MSRP LOW	MSRP HIGH	WHEN TO WEAR & MORE INFO
S/S shirt	Knit poly/merino blend or pure, 120 g/sq m weight	$20	$70	Mild temps, low sun exposure, few bugs; keep cool with air-permeability, chest zip, looser fit
L/S shirt	Same as S/S; 120–150 g/sq m weight	$30	$90	Cooler temps and/or strong sunshine; can double as bug shirt by treating with permethrin
Bug shirt	Permethrin-treated knit L/S, not a stuffy woven	$10	$100	Defense against biting insects & disease-carrying ticks, factory treatments last longer than DIY spray-ons & wash-ins
Shorts	Running shorts with silky liner, 4–6-in inseam	$20	$55	When pants are not necessary; okay as occasional underwear under pants
Trekking pants	Lightweight nylon, low spandex content	$40	$90	For protection against bugs, brush, sun, & cool temps; convertibles better in theory than practice
Underwear	Poly or merino, with spandex for fit & stretch	$15	$50	When wearing pants full-time; one pair for men, two for women; wash regularly, soap unnecessary
Fleece top	100- or 200-weight pullover, minimal features	$25	$130	As second layer in brisk conditions & as mid-layer between hiking shirt & shell when cold and wet
Shell top	Waterproof/breathable jacket with air vents	$30	$250	Delays getting wet, but ultimately fails; alternatives: poncho, umbrella, windshirt
Shell bottoms	Waterproof/breathable pants with leg zips	$50	$175	Cold precipitation; without ventilation, easy to overheat; alternatives: rain skirt, chaps, or wind pants

Insulated jacket	Premium down fill, or synthetic or 300 fleece	$50	$250	Brisk midday stops, long & cool camps, warmth at night; prefer hooded models	
Insulated pants	Down-filled with 3/4 zips, or M-65 military surplus	$20	$175	Static in cool or cold temps, notably in camp during short fall & winter days	
Sleeping top	Polyester, wool, or fleece	$0	$50	Rainy & humid trips	
Sleeping bottoms	Shorts or thermals, low performance threshold	$0	$50	Not for daytime use; store inside pack, protected; unnecessary if daytime clothes usually stay dry	
TOTAL		$310	$1,535		

FOOTWEAR

For most backpackers, traditional footwear does not achieve the best results. Boots are stiff, hot, and heavy. "Waterproof" footwear fails in prolonged wet conditions and dries very slowly. And a two-layer sock system absorbs a lot of moisture and traps a lot of heat—two of the three contributing factors to blisters.

Footwear is a very personalized category, and Skurka would encourage you to experiment until you find the optimal system for your feet and your trips.

ITEM	RANKING	MY PICK OR SUGGESTION	WEIGHT (OZ)	MSRP	COMMENTS
Shoes	Critical	Breathable trail-running or hiking shoes	12.0	$125	Vs. boots: more comfortable, faster drying, lighter, cheaper; not as durable or protective
Gaiters	Suggested	Stretch nylon, no instep	3.0	$30	Keep out dirt & debris; less necessary with pants
Hiking socks A	Critical	Merino/nylon blend	2.0	$15	Liner-like weight; more odor-resistant than poly
Hiking socks B	Depends	Same as pair A	2.0	$15	In very wet conditions, do not take; otherwise, yes
Sleeping socks	Depends	Poly, wool, or fleece	3.0	$15	Guarantee dry feet at night. Pack only if (both) daytime socks likely to get wet
Camp wear	Optional	Travel or airline slippers	1.0	$15	Avoid wearing wet (and maybe cold) shoes in camp
TOTAL			23.0	$215	

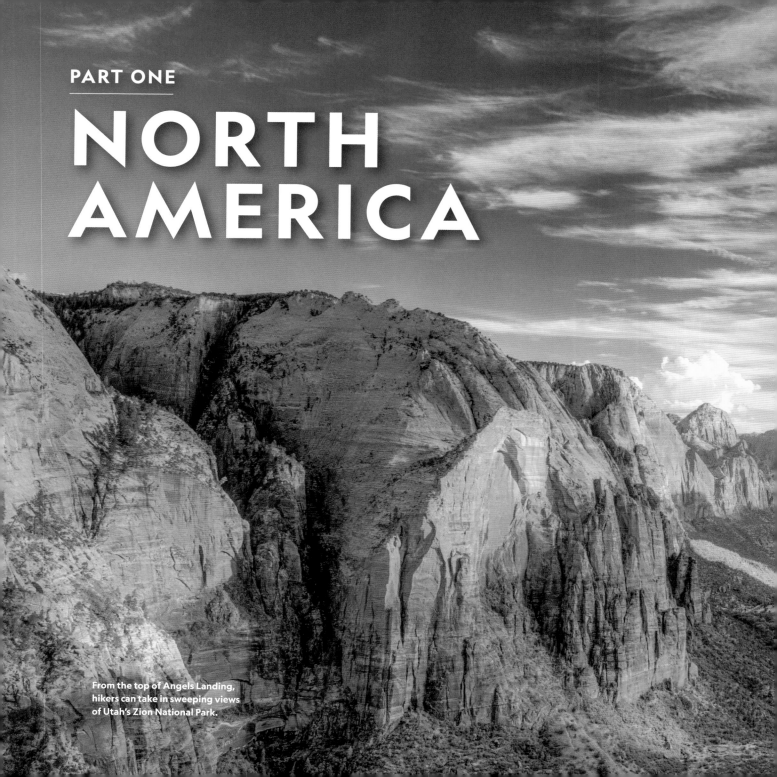

PART ONE

NORTH AMERICA

From the top of Angels Landing, hikers can take in sweeping views of Utah's Zion National Park.

HOWE SOUND CREST TRAIL

Mountains and Shore Near a Vibrant City

DISTANCE: 17 miles (28 km) point to point   **LENGTH OF TRIP: 1 to 3 days**
BEST TIME TO GO: Late summer   **DIFFICULTY: Strenuous**

Thick forests shroud many of the hills along British Columbia's shoreline, which is why the Howe Sound Crest Trail—tiptoeing across high, airy ridges—is so refreshing. Because it's within a 30-minute drive of downtown Vancouver, it has become an almighty grail for hardcore trail runners, who typically aim to tick off the 17-mile (28-km) ridgeline traverse in a day. But a two- or three-day backpack affords a comfortable, moderate (and more sane) pace to enjoy some of the most striking views of any trail on this stretch of British Columbia's coast.

The trail's head-spinning exposure is both the allure and the challenge. Most hikers attempt the trail from south to north because it presents a net loss in altitude—but don't underestimate its fierce nature. This is a rugged, difficult, mostly nonmaintained trail that requires preparedness and route-finding savvy. Starting at about 3,000 feet (900 m) in the upper parking lot of Cypress Provincial Park, the path starts off northward at a moderate incline but turns steep as it ascends St. Mark's Summit, where views of islands and the navy-colored sound unfurl far below. Over the miles, cedar and hemlock forests surrender to alpine tundra and exposed granite blocks and fins, which at times require hikers to climb hand over foot, hop between boulders, and brave thrilling (some might say stomach-turning) exposure. One of the great appeals of this route is the proximity of aesthetic peaks like

OPPOSITE: A mossy trail heads toward Deeks Lake, a preferred wilderness camping spot.

NEXT PAGES: Mount Harvey offers views of Lions Bay and Brunswick Mountain, the highest North Shore peak (5,866 feet/1,788 m).

WHAT YOU'LL SEE: Cedar and hemlock forests I Alpine tundra I Lakes I Blueberry and huckleberry thickets I Signs of bears and cougars

Mount Harvey, Unnecessary Mountain, and the Lions, which some hikers scramble up if they have extra time—and ambition.

"Once you get on top of a summit, you really feel like a mountaineer—it's very rewarding," says François-Xavier Gagnon, a mountain guide for West Coast Educational Adventures, based in North Vancouver, and a local search-and-rescue team member. "And the sunsets are amazing from everywhere. You have a mix of surf and turf—the Coast Mountains to the east and the water and the wicked sunset on the other side."

After passing Mount Brunswick, the trail descends past a series of lakes and through thickets of blueberries and huckleberries. Stop for a snack, an icy dunk, and possibly even a snooze next to a forest-rimmed pool like Deeks Lake before making the long, knee-busting journey down into the forests and to the end of the trail at Porteau Cove.

KNOW BEFORE YOU GO

The Howe Sound Crest Trail might be close to the city (just 17 miles/27 km north) but it features a challenging profile of ascents and descents. Water is scarce in comparison to lower trails, so bring plenty. And it's possible to encounter big wildlife, such as bears and cougars, along the way.

LAKE AGNES TEA HOUSE

A Hike That Includes a Cup of Tea

DISTANCE: 4.2 miles (6.8 km) out and back **LENGTH OF TRIP:** 2 to 4 hours
BEST TIME TO GO: Summer and early fall **DIFFICULTY:** Easy

In the late 19th century, the Canadian Pacific Railway built a series of hotels in the Banff, Alberta, area and beyond, including two unique teahouses high up in the wilderness, designed to serve visiting mountaineers in some of the province's most treacherous terrain. Today, the teahouses still serve legions of hikers who flock here in summer to immerse themselves in Banff National Park's glaciated peaks, gem-hued lakes, sparkling clean air, and, come July and August, meadows filled with red, purple, pink, white, and yellow wildflowers.

Lake Agnes Tea House, situated on a still alpine lake that, in windless moments, mirrors the ragged peaks beyond, first opened to visitors in 1905 and is reachable by a delightfully mellow 4.2-mile (6.8-km) round-trip hike through old-growth forest. Because it is easier and shorter than the 6.6-mile (10.6-km) round-trip hike to the Plain of Six Glaciers Teahouse, it sees the overwhelming share of visitors. Start early in the morning for the best chances of experiencing the trail in quietude.

From Chateau Lake Louise, a decadent, historic hotel on the shores of its namesake—also originally built by the Canadian Pacific Railway—the trail winds along the banks, then forks up into the forest. The first section is the most strenuous, as the path switchbacks through Engelmann spruce and Douglas fir, but small breaks in the trees offer tantalizing views of milky turquoise Lake

ALTERNATIVE ROUTE

For a more adventurous day, start with the view-heavy hike to the Plain of Six Glaciers Teahouse then loop around to Lake Agnes, a 12-mile (19-km) circuit. On the way to the first teahouse, you'll see fewer people than in the Lake Agnes area, and the views of Lefroy and Abbot Pass look as if you're hiking straight into a postcard.

OPPOSITE: Lake Agnes welcomes visitors from its perch on an alpine lake.

NEXT PAGES: The teahouse serves more than 100 types of loose leaf tea, as well as sweets like tea biscuits and jam.

Louise far below. Following the trail up, pass by Mirror Lake, then huff up past a waterfall leaking from Lake Agnes to the teahouse on its shores.

The restaurant, built of wood and stone, is a tea aficionado's nirvana, serving some 100 types of loose leaf brews as well as cookies, biscuits, soups, and sandwiches layered on fresh homemade oatmeal brown bread, all crafted from ingredients schlepped in by staff several times each week. (The staff, often high school graduates and college students, live in the teahouse's hut and in nearby cabins.) Sip your tea on the deck overlooking the quartzite walls of this dramatic hanging valley, carved by a glacier thousands of years ago, then loll about in the sunshine on the slabby rocks just outside the teahouse. Before hiking back down, climb just under a mile (1.5 km) up to the top of Big Beehive, an imposing rock formation, for a spectacular vista over Lake Louise and the rows of peaks that have lured climbers and mountaineers for well over a century.

POST-HIKE ACTIVITY

About 38 miles (60 km) southeast of Lake Louise, the tony mountain town of Banff has lured travelers for more than 100 years with its soothing mineral waters, which steam out of the earth between 98°F and 104°F (37–40°C). Go in the morning before the crowds for a peaceful soak among the evergreen trees.

LE FJORD, SAGUENAY FJORD N.P.

A Deep, Forested Inlet

DISTANCE: 26 miles (41 km) point to point   **LENGTH OF TRIP: 2 to 4 days**
BEST TIME TO GO: Summer   **DIFFICULTY: Moderate**

The Aboriginal people of Quebec called Saguenay Fjord *Pitchitao-itchez,* which roughly translates to "that which flows between two mountains," and used it as a hunting ground and gathering place. With its dramatic beauty, it's not hard to imagine why.

Today, the fjord is a national park and recreational playground. While cruise boats ply the waters and summer vacationers come in droves for the fresh air, out on the trails this place still feels ancient and primeval. Le Fjord is one of the park's prime multiday hikes, a 26-mile (41-km) ramble from Baie Sainte-Marguerite to Baie-de-Tadoussac through balsam fir and birch forests. The rocky, rolling path leads to shelters and lean-tos for sleeping, as well as passes by bald rocky alpine lookouts with expansive views over the steep-walled sound and the water some 600 vertical feet (180 m) down.

Walking through this ancient landscape, signs of life arise everywhere. Black bears patrol these forests, beavers still make their industries on shores, and peregrine falcons nest in the cliffs. (Look carefully and you might see them dive lightning-fast for prey.) Hikers also commonly spot moose, woodpeckers, and owls. And on a windless day, scan the sound for the graceful white figures of beluga whales that haunt the waters far below.

WHAT YOU'LL SEE: Balsam firs I Birch forests I Black bears I Beavers I Moose

POST-HIKE ACTIVITY

In the Baie-Éternité area of the national park, three via ferrata routes traverse the cliffs above the water. These routes feature cables and rungs, and require climbing skills and fitness—but they pay off with an even more airy view of the sound. They also include a delicate, barely there suspension bridge hovering over the water like a tightrope.

Hikers rest their feet and swap stories at the Anse-de-la-Barge refuge, open to trekkers in the summer and fall.

BROOKS RANGE TRAVERSE

A Great Arctic Wilderness

DISTANCE: Varies   **LENGTH OF TRIP:** **7-plus days**
BEST TIME TO GO: **Summer**   **DIFFICULTY:** **Expert-only**

After the bush plane leaves and the throaty hum of the engine fades into the distance, that's the moment hikers truly realize the vastness of the Brooks Range. The northernmost band of the Rocky Mountains, these peaks stretch 600 miles (nearly 1,000 km) from the Chukchi Sea to the Yukon in a brawny arm sometimes as wide as 200 miles (300 km). There are no established trails and only one lonely ribbon of road to hem you in.

"It's arguably the greatest place in North America for wilderness trekking," says Andrew Skurka, professional long-distance backpacker and National Geographic Adventurer of the Year in 2007. "You have this extremely aesthetic mountain range with incredible dramatic relief from peaks to valley. There are no trails, no bridges, no campgrounds, no gift shops—and don't expect to see people."

Naturally, hikers must be comfortable navigating overland using a map and compass or GPS. They also must be ready for the challenges of the Arctic wilderness, like wading through icy rivers, bushwhacking through thickets of willows, and hopping through fields of tussocks—maddening mounds of grass the size of five-gallon buckets.

While wandering through a landscape this gargantuan and remote may seem daunting, it's also profoundly moving to immerse oneself in such beauty,

WILDLIFE SPOTTING

Caribou herds are the lifeblood of this landscape, providing sustenance for wolves, grizzly bears, and human beings. Even golden eagles will prey on caribou calves. Hikers may encounter herds in the hundreds or—if they're supremely fortunate—in the tens of thousands, one of the planet's great wildlife spectacles.

OPPOSITE: The aurora borealis performs its magical dance over snowcapped peaks.

NEXT PAGES: The sun rises over a meadow in the traverse, highlighting its autumn colors.

which is almost entirely untouched by development. Peaks rise as high as 9,000 feet (2,700 m) in a jumble of uplifted layers as if tossed about by some giant unseen hand. Valleys stretch for an eternity and come alive with the reddish blaze of fireweed and the bronze hues of Arctic tundra plants relenting to fall. In some places, small glaciers and the signs of their artistry, such as moraines and deep valleys, grace the mountains. This is where the northernmost trees on the continent—the dwarfed, scraggly silhouettes of black spruce, paper birch, aspen, and balsam poplar—peter out into seemingly endless expanses of tundra, where only the gauziest shroud of life clings to existence.

These tiny, heroic signs of life can be lost in the enormous quietude, but they are not the only living beings here. For as long as 11,000 years, humans have carved a living out of this extreme land, from paleo-Inuit people to, more recently, Nunamiut people, among other groups. Hikers

KNOW BEFORE YOU GO

Because the Brooks Range has no trails or facilities for hikers, visitors must be highly experienced in backcountry travel and navigation. Gates of the Arctic National Park and the Arctic National Wildlife Refuge also suggest having at least one two-way communication device, such as a satellite phone. Especially for those who go in July, don't forget the head net for the mosquitoes. Bear-resistant food canisters are a must.

ABOVE: A brave trekker leaps between rocks near the Noatak River along the traverse.

OPPOSITE: Part of a large herd that calls Brooks Range home, a young caribou pauses while grazing.

often start or end their journeys in the remote villages of Alaska natives. They also find evidence of past inhabitants, too, from chert used to fashion tools to stone structures designed to weigh down the edges of skin tents.

Wildlife also sustain themselves off this land. Arctic terns arrive having flown from the Antarctic—the world's longest migration—to feast on the millions of insects that live and die in the preciously brief summer. Caribou traverse the tundra in the thousands. Listen carefully and you might hear the squeak of a ground squirrel or the howl of a distant wolf. Watch for the tracks of grizzly bears, hunting for squirrels and berries.

One of the great wonders of the Brooks Range goes beyond the land to the marvels above. In summer, the sun loops around the sky, never dipping below the horizon. And as the cold returns, so do the northern lights, which dance across the dome overhead in wondrous arcs.

COPPER CANYON

A Grander Canyon

DISTANCE: 35 miles (56 km) point to point   **LENGTH OF TRIP:** 6 to 8 days
BEST TIME TO GO: Fall   **DIFFICULTY:** Strenuous

The Grand Canyon has a monumental name and a prime reputation as a hiker's paradise, but in many respects, Mexico's Copper Canyon—a complex of six canyons plunging more than 6,000 feet (1,800 m) deep—gives it a run for its money. First of all, it's bigger and deeper. It's also home to the Tarahumara people, who have been living here for centuries and still farm, weave, and tend to orchards in this arid and dramatically beautiful landscape. Plus, to get here, a scenic train ascends more than 7,000 vertical feet (2,100 m) from the Pacific Coast to the highlands.

Most of the hikers who visit this secluded desert gem stage day hikes off the train route, visiting waterfalls tumbling hundreds of feet (tens of meters) and spending time with the locals and the Tarahumara people. But a week's tramp is the best way to immerse oneself in this unvarnished, Club Med–free corner of Mexico. The rim-to-rim-to-rim route, pioneered by the outfitter Copper Canyon Trails, follows a trail some 35 miles (56 km) and 20,000 vertical feet (6,000 m) down, up, down, and back up the canyon over seven days. Newbie hikers and pansy-foots need not apply, and the terrain is best tackled with patience and a healthy dose of humor. Many of the slopes of Copper Canyon are even steeper than the Grand Canyon's, and they can be riddled with loose fields of softball- and melon-size stones or flat rocks like broken

OPPOSITE: The Lost Cathedral is one of the many abandoned buildings left in the small town of Satevo.

NEXT PAGES: The Chihuahua-Pacific Railway traverses Copper Canyon, connecting Chihuahua to Los Mochis.

WHAT YOU'LL SEE: **Waterfalls I Goats I Oak and pine forests I Mango, papaya, and avocado trees I River Urrique I Tarahumara**

dinner plates. In other areas, spiny plants dot the path and locals' goats run to and fro. Hikers also contend with heat and aridity.

The good news is that the scenery is unequivocally outstanding. Cliffs nosedive down into the canyon, dotted with greenery and threaded with long, delicate waterfalls. Travel from pine forests down through species-rich oak forests and even farther down to areas where mango, papaya, and avocado trees grow. At the bottom of the canyon, the River Urrique is a welcome sight (and one you'll have to wade through, knee- or thigh-high, depending on the flow). You'll meet plenty of locals along the way, from Tarahumara women out collecting plants for basket-weaving to kids running around and men plowing or harvesting or building with adobe bricks. Come evening, camp by the river or a desert spring, and fall asleep to the sound of the water that is at once the creator and the lifeblood of this canyon.

KNOW BEFORE YOU GO

The U.S. State Department warns against traveling in many areas of Mexico, including Chihuahua, and drug trafficking does exist in the Copper Canyon area. In late 2018, a solo hiker was murdered by members of a drug cartel, whom he encountered on a trail. Take caution: It's wise to hire a guide who knows the area and is embedded in the community.

SIERRA HIGH ROUTE

California's Granite Kingdom

DISTANCE: 195 miles (314 km) point to point   **LENGTH OF TRIP:** 15 to 20 days
BEST TIME TO GO: Summer   **DIFFICULTY:** Expert-only

For the hiker who has done everything, high routes are the endurance test pieces of the trekking world. While they might follow trails for short segments, they are known for veering way off the beaten path on wild romps through little-frequented wilderness areas.

"On those off-trail sections, you have a map and compass and you're finding the path of least resistance between two points," says Andrew Skurka, a professional backpacker and the 2007 National Geographic Adventurer of the Year, who started doing high routes as a new skill in his backpacking repertoire in 2008. "There's a lot of thought that has to go into every footstep, but high routes go into corners of our best wilderness areas that you can't get to otherwise."

The country's first known one was the Sierra High Route, a winding north-south ribbon that runs 195 miles (314 km) along the spine of the Sierra Nevada from the South Fork of the King River to Mono Village, just northwest of Yosemite National Park. Even the most daring, seasoned hikers find a doozy of a test in this route, and it's rumored that only a few dozen complete it every year. Traveling deep into Yosemite and Sequoia & Kings Canyon National Parks, as well as the Ansel Adams and John Muir wilderness areas, the Sierra entails hair-raising Class III scrambles up sloping granite, rock-hopping across car-size boulders, post-holing up snowfields in early summer,

ALTERNATIVE ROUTE

The 215-mile (346-km) John Muir Trail is the Sierra High Route's easier (but still formidable) sibling. It parallels the higher trail, traveling lower territory in the range, connecting Yosemite National Park with Mount Whitney, the continental United States' highest peak, through plenty of Sierra wonders, from deep, earthy forests to sweeping bowls and alpine lakes.

OPPOSITE: Hikers make their way up the base of the Minarets in the center of the Ansel Adams Wilderness.

NEXT PAGES: Arrowhead Lake lies inside Kings Canyon National Park along the route.

WHAT YOU'LL SEE: Ansel Adams Wilderness I
John Muir Wilderness I Meadows I Deer I
Bighorn sheep I Marmots I Glacial tarns

and negotiating steep loose talus fields—not to mention that it only occasionally dips below 10,000 feet (3,000 m).

Although it's not far from California's dense population, it feels light-years away. The sculpted granite scenery and dizzying solitude are on a par with Alaska and other great wildernesses of the world. Climbers tramp through expansive basins of granite, such as Humphreys, where rocks and ponds poetically stud bright green meadows, all framed by a rim of serrated peaks. Fields packed with wildflowers test the boundaries of imagination with their saturated hues. And mountains dominate the sky with their ragged silhouettes. Plus, there's a reason that naturalist John Muir dubbed the Sierras the Range of Light. Glimpse alpenglow on high peaks or watch as sunbeams slant through clouds.

While much of the Sierra High Route is too high up for self-respecting bears, hikers occasionally

KNOW BEFORE YOU GO

Because the rocky scrambles of the Sierra High Route require a lot of agility, a light pack is key. Consider investing in an ultralight pack, sleeping bag, sleeping pad, and tent, and whittle your kit down to the bare essentials. Food that has low moisture content and can be rehydrated is recommended.

ABOVE: Blue Lake is a prime sunset-watching spot in the Inyo National Forest.

OPPOSITE: Finding his way, a hiker holds a compass in front of a mountain lake in the Eastern Sierra.

spot deer and bighorn sheep. In fall, mating season, the clack of their horns echoes through the cirques. Above the tree line, marmots prowl about for forage and pikas emit their high-pitched squeaks. And every afternoon in summer, thunderstorms stage their disquieting theatrics as if on cue. (For this reason, hikers typically start their days early to be able to scramble off exposed areas before 2 p.m.)

For a contrast in experiences, the Sierra High Route merges with its sibling, the John Muir Trail, from time to time. In comparison, the JMT is a superhighway of thru-hikers and the High Route a bastion of quietude (and sometimes exasperating route finding). Many high route hikers feel happy to abscond back up into the empty alpine country where they have the high cirques, glacial tarns, and starry night skies all to themselves—all the more remarkable considering it's a relative stone's throw from some of the country's most populous cities.

ANGELS LANDING, ZION N.P.

A Divine Abode

DISTANCE: 5 miles (8 km) out and back   **LENGTH OF TRIP:** 2.5 to 4 hours
BEST TIME TO GO: Spring and fall   **DIFFICULTY:** Strenuous

The charms of Zion National Park's vertiginous red-rock canyons, tucked in southern Utah, haven't been a secret for centuries. Human beings have frequented this dramatic collection of chasms for at least 10,000 years—ancestral Puebloan people built homes and granaries, Paiutes gathered and hunted, and Mormon homesteaders farmed the land. Now, visitors flock here in the thousands to see the grand results of millions of years of geological forces, and one of the most popular and renowned spots to take it all in is Angels Landing.

This aerie, atop a precipitous tower of rock in the middle of the valley, is reachable only by a challenging five-mile (8-km) round-trip trek that rises nearly 1,500 vertical feet (about 450 m) from the valley floor. From the Grotto Shuttle stop, hikers wind by the Virgin River, which continues to sculpt and deepen this canyon with its flash floods, then through Refrigerator Canyon, a cool, verdant hallway of rock carved by small tributaries. The trail leads up Walter's Wiggles, a series of switchbacks named after the park's first superintendent, Walter Ruesch, who in 1925 oversaw the hand-built construction of this trail, which was considered a feat of engineering at the time.

Scout Lookout, some 1,000 feet (305 m) over the valley floor, is a prime spot for a snack, a breathing break, and a gander at the view. Many folks turn around here because the biggest challenge lies ahead: a 400-vertical-foot

OPPOSITE: Bighorn sheep are well suited to the rocky terrain of Zion National Park.

NEXT PAGES: A hiker sits in front of Angels Landing before taking on the narrow trail to its summit.

(122-m) climb up a nerve-fraying fin of rock entirely unsuited to those who are afraid of heights. Bolted chains help steady wobbly hikers as sheer cliff faces plunge below—so steep they play host to rock climbers who scale their smooth vertical faces. But the adrenaline-spiking ascent yields a vista from the top that is incomparable: Enormous sheer, striped cliffs dotted with greenery stand sentinel over this serene valley in all directions as if regal protectors.

"This is the most classic view of Zion," says Andrew Skurka, 2007 National Geographic Adventurer of the Year. "It is especially stunning in the spring when the canyon is green. There's this contrast between the big red walls and the green grasses and the snowmelt-fed river flowing down the middle of it all." And far beyond, great monoliths recede in the distance in hues of white, pink, red, and beige.

KNOW BEFORE YOU GO

Angels Landing is exceptionally popular—with good reason—so go in the early morning or late afternoon to beat the throngs. When hiking in the desert, it's imperative to slather on sunscreen and bring a sun hat. For this hike, the Park Service recommends wearing sturdy, closed-toe, hiking shoes with grippy rubber soles for negotiating steep sandstone.

HAVASUPAI, GRAND CANYON

Turquoise Waterfall Oasis

DISTANCE: About 20 miles (32 km) out and back   **LENGTH OF TRIP:** 4 days
BEST TIME TO GO: Spring and fall   **DIFFICULTY:** Strenuous

For more than a millennium, Havasu Baaja, the people of the blue-green waters—now known as the Havasupai Tribe—have lived in a peaceful green valley embraced by terra-cotta-colored sandstone cliffs at the bottom of the Grand Canyon. This valley is blessed with a limestone aquifer that has nourished crops of beans, corn, and squash for generations. Just past the village, waterfalls tumble into travertine pools, tinted a shocking hue of turquoise, thanks to naturally occurring calcium carbonate.

This oasis amid the sandstone has been a beloved pilgrimage site for trekkers for decades. Still today, no roads pierce this canyon and the waterfalls are only accessible by a 10-mile (16-km) hike, a mule ride, or a pricey helicopter ticket. (Even the mail still arrives in the village of Supai by hoof.) That doesn't mean it's not a popular destination, however. The hike is so prized that the Havasupai Reservation runs a permitting system to manage the number of visitors.

Those hikers lucky enough to snag permits start at the western edge of the South Rim of the Grand Canyon and immediately plunge down a set of switchbacks etched into the rock all the way to the canyon floor. From there, it's a long winding walk, often shaded by the towering cliffs, to Supai and then another two miles (3.2 km) to Havasu Falls, a 97-foot (30-m)

ALTERNATIVE ROUTE

The Thunder River–Deer Creek loop, a four- to five-day route with a fraction of the visitors of Havasupai, descends into the canyon from the North Rim. Travel through millions of years of geology, past a river rocketing out of a cliff face, along the Colorado River, and to ledges in the slotlike Deer Creek Narrows.

OPPOSITE: Sandstone cliffs and green trees border the path to the Havasupai Reservation.

NEXT PAGES: Havasu Falls spills into a turquoise pool, a tropical paradise tucked away in the cliffs.

curtain of water framed by uniquely formed cliffs that almost appear as if they're melting. The turquoise pools at the bottom of the waterfall beckon to weary climbers who sunbathe on their shores.

A long, lively campground extends past Havasu Falls, following alongside the creek, and ends by Mooney Falls, an even taller cascade named after a miner who fell to his death off these cliffs. Hardy hikers brave the steep descent down to the bottom of the falls by sneaking through tunnels carved into the rock and clinging to fixed chains on steep sections. Past Mooney Falls, the crowds thin and the trail turns more rugged, but this is the greatest opportunity for solitude in the Havasu area.

The path leads down the canyon, threading alongside the creek and past waterfalls, and finally passes over the border of the reservation

THE CHALLENGE

Traveling from one rim to the other in Grand Canyon National Park is a favorite among ultrarunners and ambitious hikers. Depending on the exact routes taken, it's at least 20 miles (32 km) and some 4,500 vertical feet (nearly 1,400 m) down to the Colorado River and back up again. Some even do the "rim-to-rim-to-rim" and make the return journey on foot, avoiding a long car shuttle.

ABOVE: **A footbridge spans Havasu Creek leading to the Havasupai Indian Reservation.**

OPPOSITE: **Visitors to Havasupai must stay overnight; the campground along Havasu Creek offers reservations for three nights.**

into Grand Canyon National Park. Eight miles (13 km) from the base of Mooney Falls, it T-bones the Colorado River, where a series of ledges make perfect sunbathing spots. (On occasion, rafters even stop to offer hikers a cold drink.)

On the long journey back, savor the canyon in quiet. Listen for the lilting songs of canyon wrens. Feel the breeze against your cheeks under the shade of cottonwood trees. And marvel at the thicket of cactus gardens blooming in lipstick hues in spring.

Come evening, the campground in Havasupai Reservation is full of awed—and tuckered out—hikers. Just before nodding off, take the opportunity to stare up at the clear, star-studded skies and gape at the power of the water, wind, and other forces that created this singular, majestic cleft in the earth.

PRESIDENTIAL TRAVERSE

A Historical Footpath Through Ancient Mountains

DISTANCE: **19.8 miles (32 km) point to point**   **LENGTH OF TRIP:** **1 to 4 days**
BEST TIME TO GO: **Mid- to late summer**   **DIFFICULTY:** **Strenuous**

Underestimate the White Mountains of New Hampshire at your peril! This 87-mile-long (140-km) section of the Appalachians is within a day's drive of some of the country's biggest population centers, including Boston and New York City, but it punches far above its weight class. The range is renowned for its unpredictable weather—snowstorms, lightning, or hurricane-force winds can arrive at any month of the year. It's also renowned for its recreation: With 1,000 miles (1,600 km) of trails, spectacular exposed-rock peaks, and peaceful forests, it is a magnet for East Coast adventurers, who come in the hundreds of thousands to backpack, rock climb, trail-run, mountaineer, swim, and even ski down the steep ravines in the winter.

Arguably the most prized objective for hikers and runners is the Presidential Traverse, a 19.8-mile-plus (32-km) route connecting nine peaks named after U.S. presidents (as well as a smattering of peaks named after other people). It presents an aesthetic and irresistible challenge with some 8,500 vertical feet (2,600 m) of climbing, much of it in sensitive alpine territory above tree line. Some masochists like to tick off the entire route in one day, but take two to four to savor the views and enjoy these rare and unique ecosystems—and to allow plenty of time for bailing out down side trails if storms move in. Another reason to take multiple days is the system of tidy Appalachian

PROTECTING THE LAND

The Presidential Range is home to most of the alpine tundra in the northeastern U.S. and features tiny endemic plants that can survive wind and storms—but careless footsteps can kill them. Stay on trails and hop between rocks to protect them. Use the restroom at the huts atop Mount Washington, rather than going in alpine zones.

OPPOSITE: A member of the Mount Washington Observatory takes in the weather and landscape from the peak of Mount Washington.

NEXT PAGES: A red fox curls up among melting snow and ice on Mount Washington.

Mountain Club huts, spaced about a day's walk apart, that host hikers in bunks and feed them breakfast and dinner. (Hot soups and baked goods are available at lunchtime, too. Book months in advance for the coveted overnight reservations.)

Most people tackle the traverse from north to south, starting from the Appalachia Trailhead with a lung-busting, quadricep-squeezing ascent up Mount Madison via the Madison Springs Hut. The trail tiptoes along high alpine ridgelines as it leads to Mounts Adams, Jefferson, and Clay with views over the grand cirque of the Great Gulf Wilderness. In the middle of the trek, hikers summit Mount Washington, the highest peak in the northeast with—uncannily—a cafeteria and visitor's center at the top, a destination for some 250,000 annual visitors. (Many of them arrive by the 19th-century Cog Railway, which inches up the mountain at an unnervingly steep grade—up to 37 percent.) While the summit is most often

KNOW BEFORE YOU GO

The European-style huts that dot this route have a long, rich history of hosting hikers and mountaineers. Mizpah Springs, Lakes of the Clouds, and Madison are all conveniently located along the Presidential Traverse but require you to make reservations far ahead of time. Tent and shelter camping is also possible at some sites along the trail.

shrouded in clouds, on a sunny day it's possible to see clear over five states, Canada, and even to the Atlantic Ocean.

Some hikers spend the night at the nearby Lakes of the Clouds hut or press on past Mounts Monroe, Eisenhower, and Pierce to the Mizpah Springs Hut before heading down the Crawford Path—the oldest continuously maintained foot trail in the country, originally built in the early 1800s as a stock trail. Shuttles run by the Appalachian Mountain Club safely deposit you back at the Appalachia Trailhead.

While hikers are attracted to the Presidential Traverse for its challenge and the promise of above–tree line hiking, some of its charms lie in the quieter attractions: the small unclouded ponds that sit like mirrors between peaks, the tiny mats of alpine azalea that carve out a living in the harsh alpine zone, and the dome of salty stars that reveals itself as night falls over New England.

ABOVE: A snow-covered sign marks Mount Washington's 6,288-foot (1,917-m) summit.

OPPOSITE: Greenleaf Hut offers hot meals, trail information, and views of Mount Lafayette and Eagle Lake.

HOH RIVER TRAIL

A Cathedral of Green

DISTANCE: 34.8 miles (56 km) out and back   **LENGTH OF TRIP:** 3 to 4 days
BEST TIME TO GO: Summer   **DIFFICULTY:** Moderate

Magical. Enchanting. Straight out of a fantasy film. These are some of the ways visitors describe the Hoh, a swath of old-growth temperate rainforest on the west side of Olympic National Park, a kingdom of peaks, forests, and wild Pacific shores that encompasses much of Washington's Olympic Peninsula. This dripping repository of greenery receives some 12 to 14 feet (3.7–4.3 m) of precipitation each year, but summer consistently brings clear skies. Hikers typically arrive between June, when the high-elevation slopes are just peeling off their blanket of snow, and September, when flurries start anew. But it's possible to hike the lower-elevation area of the Hoh any time of year—provided you're ready for a good dousing.

One of the most popular footpaths through this rainforest is the Hoh River Trail, a 34.8-mile (56-km) out-and-back route that loosely follows its namesake river before heading up and out of the forests and into the high country. The trail starts off delightfully mellow, weaving by the shores of the river and then back into the forest. (Many day-hikers simply do an out-and-back on the first section of trail.) For miles, backpackers stroll through veritable hallways of green. Sitka spruce and western hemlock grow to as big as 15 feet (4.5 m) in circumference, lichens and mosses drape off their branches, and ferns and yet more moss cover every conceivable surface, making the forest floor look carpeted.

WILDLIFE SPOTTING

Olympic National Park hosts the region's biggest herd of Roosevelt elk, the largest variety of their species, and one of the best places to spot them is the Hoh Rain Forest, where they reside year-round in herds of about 20. In fall—mating season—listen for their eerie, high-pitched bugling and grunts.

OPPOSITE: It's worth pausing to take in the towering trees of the Hoh Rain Forest.
NEXT PAGES: Blue Glacier and Mount Olympus greet hikers at the end of the Hoh River Trail.

Temperate rainforest I
Roosevelt elk I **Western hemlocks** I **Sitka**
spruces I **Lichens** I **Mosses** I **Elk Lake** I **Glaciers**

The last five miles (8 km) of the trail require extra oomph as the path leads some 3,500 vertical feet (more than 1,000 m) past Elk Lake, dotted with lily pads and fringed with moss, up and out of the forests, and onto the alpine meadow slopes of Mount Olympus. The trail tops out on a lateral moraine with a view of the blue glacier, an enormous slab of ice on the north slope of this mountain, named for the abode of the gods.

Most backpackers take at least three days to get to the overlook and retrace their steps in leisurely style. After all, some of the best moments of this hike are the ones experienced in times of idleness—sitting cautiously while a bear lumbers by in the distance, watching a banana slug slowly inch across the trail, or witnessing the clouds wander up and down the slopes of this peaceful river valley, shifting, moving, and eventually disappearing into thin air.

POST-HIKE ACTIVITY

A hidden gem lies inside Alpine Lakes Wilderness Area—about a six-hour drive from the Hoh River. Gem Lake sits at the foot of Wright Mountain and can be reached by the Main Trail from Snow Lake (Gem's larger cousin) or by following the signs two miles (3.2 km) beyond the junction of Snow Lake Trail and Rock Creek Trail #1013.

KALALAU TRAIL, NAPALI COAST

A Tropical Idyll

DISTANCE: 22 miles (35 km) out and back **LENGTH OF TRIP: 1 to 3 days**
BEST TIME TO GO: Late spring and summer **DIFFICULTY: Strenuous**

From the sea, the plunging, fluted, plant-choked cliffs of Kauai's Napali Coast appear impenetrable. But native Hawaiians have been traveling through and dwelling on this forbidding shore for untold years. Today, the terraces where they once grew taro remain, and a spectacular exposed trail connects Ke'e Beach with the fabled Kalalau, a half-mile-long (nearly 1 km) spit of sand only reachable by foot or boat, ensconced in jungle and guarded by cliffs and surf. The 11-mile (18-km) one-day trek is the consummate coastal Hawaii hike.

It also has a reputation. In a few sections, hikers hold onto the roots of plants as they negotiate a narrow shelf across cliffs that plunge into the sea. (Acrophobes need not apply.) When it rains, water careens down the drainages and slopes, turning the path into a slippery mess. Sometimes flash floods swell the streams and shoot down the slopes. In the spring of 2018, floods and landslides were so strong that they damaged the route and even the highway leading to the trailhead. (In June 2019, the trail and road were repaired, and the Hawaii Department of Land and Natural Resources started to issue permits to overnight hikers—and anyone going beyond Hanakapiai Stream, at the two-mile/3.2-km mark.)

But despite its dangers—or perhaps because of them—Kalalau is intensely popular. Day-hikers clog the first few miles of the trail, but the crowds thin

OPPOSITE: An oceanside campsite offers views of the Napali Coast and Kalalau Beach.

NEXT PAGES: A day trek through the jewel-toned Napali Coast cliffs provides loads of natural wonders.

as you plunge deeper into this road-free coastline. While it's close to sea level, the trail is anything but flat, traveling up and over ridges and down into five different valleys. Natural wonders beckon at almost every turn: Waterfalls cascade down the valleys, and streams swirl into the sea. At high points, views stretch over the sailboat-dotted Pacific clear to the horizon, and the sound of crashing waves echoes far below. And then, of course, there's the grand finale: Kalalau Beach itself, a secluded swath of sand that feels positively magical after the challenges of the trek.

Hikers find campsites in the shade of the lush forest that flanks the beach, and a trail winds a couple miles up into the valley to a pool in the stream. Often, people gather to watch the light dim and the clouds turn coral over the Pacific as evening falls. Some can't bring themselves to leave and a small settlement of squatters resides here. While it's illegal to live on the beach forever, it's easy to understand why some people would try.

KNOW BEFORE YOU GO

With little warning, the streams on the Napali Coast can rise surprisingly quickly, swelling with runoff from distant rainstorms. Always wait until the flow eases before crossing—even if it means you'll miss your flight. Hikers have been injured and killed trying to cross at high water, but those who stay put witness one of the island's remarkable natural spectacles in safety.

APPALACHIAN TRAIL

The Original Long-Distance Hiking Epic

DISTANCE: 2,192 miles (about 3,528 km) point to point   **LENGTH OF TRIP:** 5 to 7 months
BEST TIME TO GO: Early spring to fall   **DIFFICULTY:** Strenuous

Among the great long-distance hiking-only footpaths of the world, the Appalachian Trail is the longest and arguably the most storied. The brainchild of an idealistic forester named Benton MacKaye, the trail was completed in 1937 as an antidote to the buzz of an increasingly industrializing Eastern Seaboard. Now, the relative quietude of the trail, a slim ribbon of wilderness through some of the most densely populated regions of the United States, has perhaps never been more precious and needed.

Running along the crest of the Appalachian Mountains like a parenthesis to the East's big coastal cities, the AT, as it is affectionately known, stretches about 2,192 miles (about 3,528 km) from Katahdin in Maine to Springer Mountain in northern Georgia. These eastern mountains are elderly by mountain-range standards and barely top 6,000 feet (1,800 m) at their highest. Perhaps because of the trail's proximity to civilization, it is easy to underestimate. But among the more than 4,000 people who attempt to walk the entire thing each year, only about one in four makes it.

In some areas, the trail beelines straight up a peak, only to plunge off the other side and right back down. Seasoned hikers refer to these bemusedly as PUDs—or pointless ups and downs. In other areas, such as the Mahoosuc Notch, in Maine, walkers clamber hand over foot monkey-style over a solid

ALTERNATIVE ROUTE

While thousands attempt to hike the entire trail each year, the Appalachian Trail Conservancy estimates that some three million people use it, most as day-hikers. Great day-size chunks of trail abound. In the Roan Highlands of Tennessee, huff up to a treeless summit known as a "bald" for views over bucolic farmland.

OPPOSITE: Rhododendrons bloom along the Roan Highlands on the border of Tennessee and North Carolina.

NEXT PAGES: Only about one in four thru-hikers completes the entire 2,192-mile (3,528-km) Appalachian Trail.

mile (1.5 km) of boulders, ranging in size from marbles to motorboats. Perhaps the biggest challenge, however, is the monotony of mile after mile of leafy green tunnels of lush deciduous forests.

And yet, this trail commands a loyal, even fervid, following. Its payoffs include airy outcroppings with views of blue-hued mountains, the sight of a deer nursing a freshly born fawn, and the murmuring of a peaceful stream cascading over moss-framed rocks deep in the woods.

For many, the fact that this trail is historic and beloved is a large draw—fellow hikers form a tight community, swapping advice, stories, and food. They often even fondly give each other trail names— Rodeo Clown, Thunder Chicken, Lost and Found— as they negotiate a profound physical challenge. And, naturally, when they come to the end—for most, that is the top of the fearsome Katahdin of Maine—they cheer and cry and laugh together.

KNOW BEFORE YOU GO

Because so many people attempt the trail from south to north every year, the southern sections get overcrowded. Consider "flip-flopping," the practice of starting in the middle of the trail somewhere, finishing, then tackling the remainder of the trek at the end. The Appalachian Trail Conservancy, the nonprofit that cares for the trail, offers workshops and advice for thru-hikers.

WAITUKUBULI NATIONAL TRAIL

The Jungle Adventure

DISTANCE: 115 miles (185 km) point to point   **LENGTH OF TRIP:** 10 to 14 days
BEST TIME TO GO: Spring, summer, and winter   **DIFFICULTY:** Expert-only

While many Caribbean islands have sprouted a pox of all-inclusive resorts and beachside development, Dominica has remained relatively unscathed, thanks to its precipitous shores; small, hair-raising runway; and dearth of white sandy beaches. (Its few beaches are of the cobble and black-sand variety.) As a result, this series of volcanic knobs, self-branded as the "nature island," is blissfully unpretentious and full of spots to immerse yourself in the natural world and a rich Caribbean culture.

Small inns and a few resorts have sprung up on the coasts, but tourism has come slowly to the interior of the island, the home of the Kalinago people, who have lived here since before Europeans arrived. The Waitukubuli National Trail, which opened in 2013, was built partly as an effort to bring visitors to these small, interior communities and to show off attractions like hot springs, 4,000-foot (1,200-m) peaks, and cliff-secluded beaches. The first long-distance hiking trail in the region, it snakes 115 miles (185 km) from Scotts Head Peninsula—a pleasing stretch of coastline with a smattering of inns and restaurants—northward, grazing the eastern shore of the island then sweeping northwest to its terminus at Cabrits National Park.

While the trail is well signed, don't come here expecting a tidy national park–like experience. This is not an adventure you'll be able to script. Waitukubuli

OPPOSITE: The ruins of the Commandant's Quarters at Fort Shirley are covered in forest overgrowth.

NEXT PAGES: Stone carvings decorate Kalinago Barana Autê, an interpretive center that showcases Dominica's first peoples' traditions.

WHAT YOU'LL SEE: Rainforest I Waterfalls I Cliff-rimmed beaches I Natural hot springs I Cinnamon trees I Sisserou and Jaco parrots I Mango trees

presents many challenges, from steep, slippery slopes to sweltering heat to sections littered with babyhead cobbles. From time to time, the sky unleashes vigorous downpours on unsuspecting hikers, swelling the rivers and waterfalls. On occasion, landslides take out parts of the trail—2017's Hurricane Maria dealt blows to all 14 sections, which are still being rebuilt. And the culture is refreshingly laid-back. (In other words, not for obsessive planners.) It's not uncommon for hikers to arrange transport and lodging last-minute by simply calling up a local who offers rides or a homestay.

Naturally, for some, the adventurousness of the experience is a large part of the draw. And the mud-soaked slogs through thick tunnels of greenery yield fascinating rewards, from eye-popping views over the sea to an immersion in Kalinago territory—Dominica has the largest population of indigenous people in the region—to Emerald Pool, where a sinuous waterfall plunges into a perfect turquoise pond, ripe for dipping.

KNOW BEFORE YOU GO

Along much of the trail, locals have opened hostels and homestays and even sell hot meals (and occasionally moonshine) by the road. The Kalinago people farm cassava and bake fresh cassava bread, available for purchase. And the trail itself abounds in natural wonders: Cinnamon scents the forest, and hikers can pluck fresh mangoes from wild trees.

LONGS PEAK CLIMB

Bagging a Fourteener

DISTANCE: 15 miles (24 km) out and back   **LENGTH OF TRIP: 10 to 15 hours**
BEST TIME TO GO: Late summer   **DIFFICULTY: Strenuous**

Colorado boasts more terrain above 10,000 feet (3,048 m) than any other state in the contiguous United States, with more than 50 peaks rising over 14,000 feet (4,300 m). Ticking off every one of them has become a prized goal among die-hard hikers, climbers, and even skiers, who, in recent years, have vied to set the speediest records. Among these lofty objectives, Longs Peak, with its regal faces, giant bulk, and proximity to Denver—only 75 miles (120 km) northwest of the city—calls a siren song to climbers across the West.

Skewering the steady blue Colorado sky at 14,259 feet (4,350 m), Longs looms over all the other peaks in Rocky Mountain National Park, a bastion of vertical rock, conifer forests, alpine tundra, and even a few small glaciers. The peak attracts an estimated 15,000 hopeful summiteers annually. Amazingly, more than half don't make the summit because of fatigue, altitude sickness, or foul weather. (And park rangers are often called to rescue people who have planned poorly or made bad decisions—the hike and the conditions should not be underestimated.) But play your cards right and it can be an enjoyable challenge.

For the best chances at a successful summit bid along the Keyhole Route—the most popular way—savvy hikers start as early as two in the morning in order to tag the top and get back down to tree line safely before afternoon

OPPOSITE: Chasm Lake sits at 11,803 feet (3,597.5 m) above sea level in the shadow of Longs Peak.

NEXT PAGES: Nearly 15,000 summiteers attempt Longs Peak every year, each hoping to add a fourteener to their list.

thunderstorms sweep through—a common occurrence in the summer months.

Long before sunrise, the climb starts off serene as you make your way along a buffed trail through forest in the dark stillness of predawn. As sunlight brightens the sky, you'll pass the sheer Diamond Face, a fearsome wall on the peak's eastern side that lures rock climbers, then scoot past an alpine lake and up a field full of ankle-twisting boulders to the telltale keyhole-like formation that bequeaths the route its name. From there, the trail leads to The Ledges, a series of very narrow shelves along a cliff edge, and The Trough, a steep gully full of loose rock, to The Narrows, a queasy-making ledgelike path that crosses a sheer cliff face. A slick granite slab is then the only thing between you and the summit. Scamper (carefully) up the sloping rock, following the painted bull's-eye trail markers to the wide, rocky summit, where a glorious tableau of Rocky Mountains unwinds below, topped by Colorado's characteristic blue dome.

ALTERNATIVE ROUTE

Because they're the highest, the Colorado fourteeners get all the glory. But this state also has a panoply of 13,000-foot (4,000-m) peaks that are far less frequented than their slightly higher siblings. Find solitude on a thirteener like Twilight, a dark, sharky fin that rises from the Weminuche Wilderness north of Durango.

HARDING ICEFIELD TRAIL

A Colossus of Ice in Kenai Fjords National Park

DISTANCE: 8.2 miles (13.2 km) out and back
BEST TIME TO GO: Late summer to early fall
LENGTH OF TRIP: 5 to 7 hours
DIFFICULTY: Strenuous

The Harding Icefield extends over some 700 square miles (1,800 sq km) of Alaska's southern Kenai Peninsula. From above, it appears as an endless swirling monochrome of white, flanked by the elegant gray-flecked arms of glaciers that descend into the sea, lakes, or land. More than one thousand feet (304.8 m) thick, the icefield is a force of nature, so big and cold that it influences the area's temperatures, winds, and even pressure systems.

Among the world's great icefields, Harding also happens to be one of the easiest to see up close—namely, by traveling 8.2 miles (13.2 km) out and back along the Harding Icefield Trail, a steep, rugged huff up some 3,000 vertical feet (900 m) of switchbacks and rolling trail. From the ranger station in the valley, the path snakes through alder and cottonwood stands, past meadows freckled with hardy wildflowers and dyed with greenish heather, to a kingly lookout. Here, hikers can behold an expanse of ice that makes them feel microscopic. Even with all that ice, *nunataks,* a word for "lonely peaks" in an Inuit language, pierce through and punctuate the whiteness with the deep black rock. On the way back down, keep on the lookout for one of Alaska's other famed phenomena—black bears, who like to feast on salmonberries that fringe the trail.

WHAT YOU'LL SEE: Glaciers I Icefields I Cottonwoods I Wildflowers I Salmonberries

PROTECTING THE LAND

Delicate alpine plants may be able to withstand plunging temperatures, high winds, and fierce storms, but lots of foot traffic is a unique challenge. Protect these fierce little flora and prevent erosion by staying on the trail and refraining from cutting new switchbacks.

Hardy mountain goats, actually part of the antelope family, can be spotted in the hills surrounding the Icefield Trail.

ACATENANGO VOLCANO

A Fiery Summit

DISTANCE: **9 miles (14.5 km) out and back**   LENGTH OF TRIP: **1 to 2 days**
BEST TIME TO GO: **Late fall through early spring**   DIFFICULTY: **Moderate**

From the Mexican border, a row of dozens of volcanoes snakes 180 miles (nearly 300 km) through southern Guatemala, clear to El Salvador. Several of these beasts loom above the colonial city of Antigua, and one, Fuego, still actively rumbles and spouts smoke and fire. One of the best ways to see its mind-blowing force is by climbing its peaceful, dormant neighbor, 13,045-foot (4,000-m) Acatenango.

The approximately nine-mile (14.5-km) round-trip journey up Acatenango's flanks has become a beloved hike among visitors, some of whom huff it out in one long day. But an overnight hike allows for a camping break mid-slope with views of nearby Volcan Fuego, which performs a spectacular natural fireworks show almost nightly—a phenomenon best seen under a blanket of darkness.

The route is well trod and climbs through four distinct microclimates. Climb through local farmers' fields of lilies, corn, and beans; old-growth cloud forest; pine woods; and finally up a barren summit cone of loose rock to the top, where views over mighty volcanoes, countryside, and even Lake Atitlán and its three volcanoes unfold before you, sometimes dotted with fluffy cobblestone-like clouds far below. Don't be surprised if Fuego once again steals the show with plumes of magnificent smoke and impressive roars.

WHAT YOU'LL SEE: **Four volcanoes I Fields of lilies I Cloud forest I Lake Atitlán**

KNOW BEFORE YOU GO

Hikers have occasionally become lost or succumbed to the elements on Acatenango, so consider hiring a guide, either through an outfitter in Antigua, such as Old Town Outfitters, or by arranging a private local guide in La Soledad, the gateway town. It can also be surprisingly cool and windy at the peak, so bring warm layers.

From the top of dormant Acatenango, climbers watch plumes of ashy smoke erupt from nearby Fuego volcano.

CORCOVADO NATIONAL PARK

A Wildlife Cornucopia

DISTANCE: 24 miles (40 km) point to point   **LENGTH OF TRIP: 2 to 3 days**
BEST TIME TO GO: Winter through mid-spring   **DIFFICULTY: Moderate**

Much of Latin America's Pacific Coast is dry because of the prevailing weather patterns, but on Costa Rica's southern shore, the wind swirls around the Cordillera de Talamanca, picks up moisture from the sea, and drops it right over the Osa Peninsula. The result is the largest intact swath of lowland Pacific rainforest in Central America—a bastion of deep, lush, wet, vine-choked woods and empty gray-sand beaches. Thankfully, forward-thinking Costa Ricans set aside much of the peninsula as a renowned national park, Corcovado, where species that have been endangered or extirpated elsewhere thrive.

The best way to see the abundant wildlife is undoubtedly on foot. From the grungy hippie gateway town of Puerto Jimenez, hikers travel by car to the end of the road at Carate, then walk 12 miles (19 km) through jungle punctuated with lookouts over the ocean. Along the way, listen to the startling, eerie sounds of howler monkeys and the chirps, squawks, and whirrs of birds as you make your way to Sirena, a biological station on the coast that offers bunk beds and meals to hikers. After spending the night—or two or three—hikers either backtrack or walk another 12 miles (19 km) through the meaty interior of the park to the end of the road at Los Patos.

To see the most critters, take your time and move slowly. It's not uncommon to spot species that are virtually impossible to see anywhere else, like

OPPOSITE: Corcovado National Park covers nearly half of the Osa Peninsula, protecting more than 163 square miles (422 sq km) of lowland tropical rainforest.

NEXT PAGES: Scarlet macaws are just one of many species that earned Corcovado the National Geographic title of "most biologically intense place on Earth."

WHAT YOU'LL SEE: Tapirs I Bull sharks I Crocodiles I Spider monkeys I Anteaters I Coatis I Ocelots I Pumas I Frogs I Scarlet macaws I Butterflies

tapirs that often browse peacefully on the grassy meadows outside of the biological station. In the Rio Sirena, bull sharks occasionally swim close to the surface looking for prey, and crocodiles bask on the shores. In the forest, spider monkeys swing from tree to tree, endangered anteaters prowl about, and coatis (little pointy-snouted, striped-tail raccoon relatives) scurry around in families. Those who are exceedingly lucky might even spot some of the country's last remaining wild cats, including ocelots and pumas. But even the small wildlife here is charismatic, from the multicolored frogs and scarlet macaws to the lovely ethereal butterflies that waft through.

The way to Sirena takes a good eight hours and sneaks in and out of the forest and along the coast. The weather is often heavily humid and warm, making a good stash of water necessary—and regular dips in creeks a must. But this sweat-fest of a hike pays off handsomely in wildlife sightings—and the unmarred, civilization-free view over the Pacific at Sirena makes for a soothing finale.

POST-HIKE ACTIVITY

While the Osa Peninsula's interior is known for animals, its shores are known for surf. Local outfitters and resorts offer lessons and rentals on the peninsula itself. Across the gulf on the very southern coast of Costa Rica, Pavones is a laid-back surf town with a left-hand break that stretches for more than half a mile (about 1 km).

TETON CREST TRAIL

Peaks, Wildlife, and Wilderness

DISTANCE: About 35 miles (56 km) point to point   **LENGTH OF TRIP:** 4 to 5 days
BEST TIME TO GO: Summer   **DIFFICULTY:** Strenuous

The unmistakable visages of the Tetons loom over Grand Teton National Park's Jenny Lake like intimidating deities. It's a classic mountain vista that has been photographed by Ansel Adams and countless visitors over the years, but unknown to the car-driving masses, there are arguably even better views from the backside. And the way to access them is via the Teton Crest Trail, one of the country's premier wilderness treks.

Linking together about 35 miles (56 km) of trails—depending on the exact route you choose—through Bridger-Teton National Forest and Grand Teton National Park, this path leads through high alpine scenery fit for royalty: fields bursting with wildflowers, dark peaks spearing the sky, bucolic lakes hidden in high valleys, and a preponderance of big wildlife that sets it apart from just about any other part of the contiguous United States.

This is a landscape that still has all the species that roamed here when indigenous people were the sole inhabitants of the land. It's not uncommon to see black and grizzly bears, moose, deer, and marmots. Although they are rare to see, even elusive wolverines, lynx, and mountain lions also patrol these high mountain haunts.

Many people start the hike by taking Jackson Hole Mountain Resort's tram, which deposits hikers more than 4,000 feet (1,200 m) up in a matter of 20 minutes (plus there is a waffle stand at the top). Then they follow the route

OPPOSITE: Fog hovers below the peaks after a rainstorm clears from upper Paintbrush Canyon.

NEXT PAGES: Bull moose are found in high concentrations around Grand Teton National Park.

north to Paintbrush Canyon. The trail often winds above tree line, affording primo views of the range and memorable campsites. Set up for the night on a tent platform on the shores of Marion Lake, ensconced in wildflower meadows and guarded by a sentry-like monolith. On the Death Canyon Shelf, fall asleep in a nook overlooking an expansive canyon striped with cliff bands. In Alaska Basin, watch as the alpenglow fades off the peaks on a midsummer evening and the still water of high lakes reflects the colors of the sunset. Traveling south to north, hikers save the best for last, careening west around the Grand Teton, Middle Teton, and Mount Owen. The hike up from Lake Solitude to Paintbrush Divide involves some 1,500 vertical feet (450 m) of high-altitude switch-backs, but you'll reap outrageous views of these massive, domineering peaks. For a relatively short investment of time—most people do the trail in less than a week—it's an incommensurate reward.

WILDLIFE SPOTTING

Black and grizzly bears are common in the Tetons, which is why the Park Service requires hikers to carry bear canisters and bear spray. But moose are another animal to be aware of. Often they simply mind their business, but occasionally, they can become aggressive. Back away, and if the moose charges, try to get behind a rock or a tree.

PART TWO

SOUTH AMERICA

Remarkably tall wax palm trees (197 feet/
60 m) dot the landscape of the Valle de
Cocora trek in Colombia (page 136).

SALKANTAY TREK

The Alternative Route to Machu Picchu

DISTANCE: **46 miles (74 km) point to point** **LENGTH OF TRIP:** **4 to 6 days**
BEST TIME TO GO: **Austral fall through spring** **DIFFICULTY:** **Strenuous**

Since it was rediscovered by Hiram Bingham in 1911, the ancient Inca city of Machu Picchu has inspired mystical reverence and spurred many starry-eyed history buffs to pilgrimage to the site over the decades. So many, in fact, that the Inca Trail, which leads to these ruins—perched scenically between two peaks at about 7,700 feet (2,300 m) in the Cordillera de Vilcabamba of the Peruvian Andes—has become clogged with tourists. Now, the Peruvian government hands out "only" 500 permits to hikers each day. As a result, a small cottage industry of alternative routes has sprouted in the region around Cusco and the Sacred Valley, including the stunning Salkantay Trek.

Travelers typically fly into Cusco, once the capital of the Inca civilization and considered one of the oldest continuously inhabited cities in the hemisphere. Situated at about 11,000 feet (3,400 m), it also makes a good place to acclimate for a few days. Check out centuries-old stone walls, and meet local people dressed in colorful woven attire.

The Salkantay Trek starts from a trailhead outside of Soraypampa, about a couple hours' drive from Cusco, through a parade of mountains, passes, and more than a dozen different ecosystems to end at a station where a train whisks hikers to Aguas Calientes, the gateway to Machu Picchu. Along the way, hikers are struck by the immensity of the peaks and glaciers, the

KNOW BEFORE YOU GO

If you'd like to follow in the Inca's footsteps, you'll probably be topping out at well over 10,000 feet (3,000 m). It's wise to set aside a few days to acclimate during your trip and stay well hydrated. Be aware of the symptoms of altitude sickness—headache, nausea, dizziness, fatigue—and always descend if they worsen.

OPPOSITE: A rocky path leads to the Inca ruins of Ollantaytambo.

NEXT PAGES: Along the Salkantay Trek, Humantay Lake is a great spot to stop for lunch.

warmth of the people who dwell in these mountains, and the wide diversity of landscapes, from high alpine zones to cloud forests and stands of bamboo. As the days pass, hikers also stop at various archaeological sites and at Humantay Lake with its brilliant turquoise hue. While it's possible to camp, many choose to stay in a string of swanky high-altitude ecolodges situated a day's walk apart and run by Mountain Lodges of Peru. (No doubt, some creature comforts are enticing after days walking above 12,000 feet/3,600 m). The most challenging part of the trek is generally considered to be Salkantay Pass, which looms over 15,000 feet (4,600 m). After that, the trek heads downhill for some time, plowing through boulder fields, rolling hills, river valleys, and cloud forests. Before reaching Aguas Calientes, hikers climb and descend Llactapata Pass and the

ALTERNATIVE ROUTE

Another alternative to the Inca Trail is the Lares Trek, which is typically done in three to four days. Hikers schlep over several high passes—the highest tops 14,000 feet (4,300 m)—and glance up at views of toothy Ausungate. Weave through remote mountain communities, past small lakes and agricultural fields and herds of grazing alpacas before reaching the ruins of Ollantaytambo and transferring by train and bus to Machu Picchu.

eponymous ruins, from which one can see a unique backdoor view of Machu Picchu.

"There are so many highlights along the trail that it's hard to say which is my favorite," says Andres Adasme, a program developer for Mountain Lodges of Peru. "It is probably the majesty of the beautiful Salkantay mountain or the pristine waters of the sacred Humantay Lake. Some will say it is the amazing contrasts and diversity you can experience, from glaciers to high cloud forest—or just to feel the sensation of having your feet over an ancient Inca trail."

And, naturally, Machu Picchu itself is a fitting reward: Situated in a narrow saddle between steep green thumbs, it is among the few pre-Columbian ruins that remains virtually entirely intact. It's not hard to imagine what it must have been like to live here centuries ago perched high in these sacred mountains, ensconced in visiting clouds.

ABOVE: Reaching Machu Picchu, trekkers find Inca ruins including stone terraces and a watcher's hut.

OPPOSITE: Hikers are often welcomed by the local people who dwell in the mountains that they ascend along the trail.

TAMBOPATA NATIONAL RESERVE

A Haven for Wild Creatures

DISTANCE: Varies   LENGTH OF TRIP: 1-plus days
BEST TIME TO GO: April through November   DIFFICULTY: Easy

There are no big highways or roads or even well-maintained national scenic trails that traverse the jungles of Tambopata National Reserve, a 678,774-acre (271,510-ha) tract of pristine old-growth forest along the banks of the Tambopata River in the lowlands of Peru. But there are slim footpaths that wrestle through the greenery, offering intrepid hikers a full immersion in the jungle.

Hikers typically see this forest by staying in small ecolodges that dot the Tambopata River, a long, lazy, chocolatey thoroughfare that serves as the region's de facto highway. Among the ecolodges in the area, Tambopata Research Center is the most tucked away and is the only lodge that sits inside the boundaries of the reserve itself. (A scientific research station, it was established in 1990 and was grandfathered in when the reserve was established in 2000.)

Amble through thick jungle dominated by kapok trees with enormous buttressed roots and palms with leaves big enough to wrap an entire person. Explore a palm swamp with trunks that soar 100 feet (30.5 m) into the air, a bamboo forest, or a clay lick where hundreds of Technicolor macaws come to get their mineral salts—and socialize, of course.

Hikes from Tambopata reward a slow pace, quietude, and peaceful alertness. If you have the eyes and the patience, a whole universe of wildlife hides

OPPOSITE: **A canopy walkway hovers 70 feet (21 m) above the rainforest floor.**

NEXT PAGES: **Capybaras and giant cowbirds are among the diverse wildlife found in Tambopata National Reserve.**

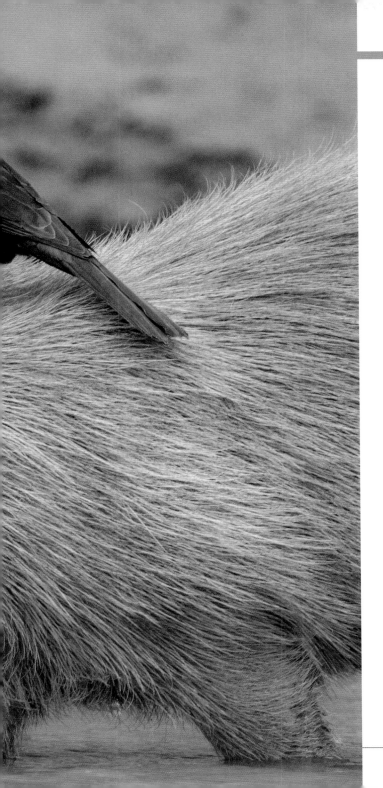

WHAT YOU'LL SEE: Tambopata River I Kapok trees I Palm swamp I Bamboo forests I Macaws I Squirrel monkeys I Peccaries I Capybaras I Parrots I Parakeets I Toucans I Hummingbirds

in plain sight. It's not uncommon to see a troupe of squirrel monkeys swinging through the trees or a herd of up to 60 peccaries careening through the underbrush. Along the banks of the river, capybaras—the world's largest rodents, which resemble sheep-size guinea pigs—poke around for roughage to eat. And overhead, parrots, parakeets, toucans, and hummingbirds fill the forest with song. In small oxbow lakes, it's even possible to spot giant river otters as they gracefully arc through the still waters. While they are elusive, jaguars also occasionally show themselves to visitors traveling by boat and even on foot.

After a long day of walking up and down through rugged and sometimes muddy terrain in the lowland heat and humidity, fall asleep to the sounds of the jungle in an open-air room. With the jungle constantly in dynamic flux, each new day brings a new path through the greenery, new surprises, and new discoveries.

ALTERNATIVE ROUTE

Come evening, the rainforest transforms. Birds, mammals, and insects call into the dark, and the beam of a flashlight reveals sets of glowing eyes staring back from the bush. Consider a night hike to look for species that emerge in the evening, from small mammals peering down from trees to frogs, tarantulas, and glowworms dwelling on the forest floor.

W TREK, TORRES DEL PAINE

Patagonia's Iconic Towers

DISTANCE: About 50 miles (about 80 km) point to point   **LENGTH OF TRIP:** 4 to 5 days
BEST TIME TO GO: Austral spring, summer, and fall   **DIFFICULTY:** Moderate

The W Trek, named for its loosely W-shaped route, is one of Patagonia's most popular treks—and with good reason. Torres del Paine National Park has one of the world's greatest collections of soaring granite monoliths, so sharp and vertiginous they test the limits of credulity. And the W Trek threads right through the midst of the most iconic ones.

It can be quite a journey to get to the W from just about anywhere in the Western Hemisphere. Tucked deep in Chilean Patagonia, it requires international flights to either Buenos Aires or Santiago, domestic flights to Punta Arenas or El Calafate, and then a couple of bus rides to top it all off. Yet the schlep is undoubtedly worth the scenery that awaits.

If you're traveling from east to west, as most hikers do, the first day is an immediate crowd pleaser. You'll climb up through a forest of slim, deciduous lenga trees to the Mirador Torres, which deposits you right at the base of an audience of soaring towers high over a green lagoon. The next day, a mellower walk leads by expansive, strikingly aquamarine Nordenskjöld Lake where views sweep over peaks and hanging glaciers. Keep an eye out for giant condors circling effortlessly overhead or guanacos, llama-like mammals, as you make your way to Los Cuernos, a *refugio* reachable only on foot. (Its charming private cabins, each nestled into a hillside and

WILDLIFE SPOTTING

Thanks to local conservation efforts, pumas have staged a comeback in recent years. While they were once highly elusive, hikers now spot them more often, particularly in low-traffic times of the year. The pumas are typically preoccupied with hunting hares, but, just in case, don't turn your back on them for a selfie.

OPPOSITE: Grey Glacier, part of the Southern Patagonian Ice Field, is 98 feet (30 m) high at its peak.

NEXT PAGES: Hikers make their way toward Lake Nordenskjöld, a picturesque stop.

equipped with wood-burning stoves and porches with vistas of craggy granite fins, are a favorite among hikers.) From there, the trail leads to a lookout over the Frances Glacier and eventually to Mirador Britanico, a viewpoint where you can stand beneath and marvel at a ring of imperious horns, buttresses, and steeples. On the last day, climb up to the Grey Glacier Lookout to see the blue-tinted mass of glacial ice presiding over a dark lagoon, backed by often-snowy peaks in the distance.

The weather in Patagonia is famous for its fierce winds and unexpected storms, but in the warm months, it can also heat up. Most hikers tackle the trail during the Southern Hemisphere's summer, between about December and February, which means that the trail can be quite crowded. Then again, the social aspect of the trail is part of the fun. Hikers often gather in the evenings over a hot meal or *cerveza* in the refugios that dot the trail

ALTERNATIVE ROUTE

For those with a little more time—and backpacking equipment—consider the longer, approximately eight-day route that travels the W but then tacks on several days connecting the ends in a magnificent loop through the backcountry with an immersion in glaciers, lakes, lenga forests, and, of course, the park's signature towers and fins.

ABOVE: Trekkers can camp, eat, and rest at El Chileno Refuge in Las Torres.

OPPOSITE: Guanacos' warm wool allows them to withstand the cold Torres del Paine climate.

to swap stories about the day's walk or other South American travels. The outposts are a welcome sight after a long day of walking. (It's also possible to camp along the trail.)

To avoid crowds, some hikers choose to come in the shoulder seasons. For more solitude, go in austral winter, between about May and September, when colder temperatures and calmer breezes arrive. This is when the park sleeps quietly under a mantle of snow—enough to frost the peaks but generally only about a foot or less on the trails. With fewer visitors, it's also easier to spot elusive wildlife, such as pumas on the hunt for small mammals.

"As a guide in the park for 15 years, winter was the time I re-fell in love with Torres del Paine," says Sergio Nuñez, a director of One Seed Expeditions, which guides winter hikes in the park. "There's the drama of the snow and the stone. The light is lower and lower, and the best sunsets and sunrises are in winter."

DIENTES DE NAVARINO CIRCUIT

The World's Southernmost Hiking Circuit

DISTANCE: 33 miles (53 km) point to point **LENGTH OF TRIP: 3 to 4 days**
BEST TIME TO GO: Austral summer **DIFFICULTY: Expert-only**

Patagonia is so full of eye-popping treks that it can be hard to choose which one to tackle first. If you're in the market for an immersion in wildness, the Dientes de Navarino Circuit stands out. The island of Navarino is situated on the southernmost tip of South America, and even getting to Puerto Williams, the island's only town, can feel like a pilgrimage to the end of the planet. But consider that the indigenous Yagan people called this seemingly inhospitable place, defined by weather and strong winds, home for some 10,000 years, living successfully off the abundance of the sea before Europeans arrived and shivered under their woolen blankets. For most of us, a foray into the belly of Navarino along this tenuous footpath is a humbling encounter with the extremes of the Earth.

"This hike is intense not because of the number of kilometers," says Vicky Jensen, an Argentine trip manager at Adventure Life, who hiked the trail for the first time in 2017. "It's intense because of the wild and remote area, weather, and the surroundings."

It's essential for trekkers who undertake the Dientes Circuit to be well equipped with layers and have plenty of hiking experience. The trail starts off winding through beautiful southern beech forests then goes through peat bogs and barren, rocky slopes, sculpted by glaciers and chiseled by wind. Over three to four days, trekkers labor up three passes, saving the

OPPOSITE: Alpine flowers bloom on Navarino Island, south of the Beagle Channel.

NEXT PAGES: The Navarino Circuit offers vistas of sweeping mountain ranges and tree-dotted landscapes.

highest, 2,772-foot (845-m) Virginia Pass, for last while passing by countless limpid lagoons that appear like clear eyes gazing upon the sky above.

Because it often rains, some of the route is full of ankle-deep muck. Other sections are marked by steep hillsides covered in loose cobbles or shifting gravel. Not a whole lot of fauna survives here, but you might find Magellanic woodpeckers or beavers—and, of course, lichens, mosses, and liverworts. Nonetheless, the landscape has a dramatic beauty that speaks for itself. Toothy peaks jut out of the earth, looming like hooded medieval figures against the often-milky sky. Pools of water sit so still one can see clear to the multicolored stones on the bottom as if looking through air. And an immersion in the windy conditions, shifting storms, and cold temperatures—usually in the 30s Fahrenheit at night (about 0°C) and the 50s Fahrenheit (10+°C) during the day in summertime—of this edge-of-a-continent trek can inspire a new reverence for the powerful forces of this wild planet.

POST-HIKE ACTIVITY

In Puerto Williams, the Martin Gusinde Anthropological Museum claims the honor of being the southernmost museum in the world. Learn about the Yagan people, other canoe-faring indigenous inhabitants of Tierra del Fuego, and the history of European visitation and settlement through maps, artifacts, and displays.

VALLE DE LA LUNA

Valley of the Moon in the Atacama Desert

DISTANCE: Varies   LENGTH OF TRIP: 1 day
BEST TIME TO GO: Austral spring, summer, and fall   DIFFICULTY: Easy

The driest place on Earth might not sound particularly inviting, but the Atacama Desert is blessed with a different kind of abundance. This otherworldly landscape, high up on a Chilean plateau west of the Andes Mountains, is full of canyons, hoodoos, salt caves, and other mysterious geological formations. Vast landscapes tinted variations of crimson, burnt sienna, beige, and ocher stretch for miles, stark against a rich blue sky. For a one-day immersion in the best of these unusual lands, it's hard to beat Valle de la Luna, also known as Valley of the Moon, about eight miles (13 km) west of San Pedro de Atacama, a bustling tourist town.

There aren't exactly trails in Valle de la Luna—an open expanse rimmed with terra-cotta-hued cliffs. A hike here is more like a meditative perambulation, an opportunity for musing on the strange wonders this planet can create in all of its endless fluxes. While there's no dearth of visitors, it's still easy, in such an expansive area, to feel a sense of quietude. Over several hours, stroll around a great amphitheater with bright-red rock formations and swaths of sand. Visit the salt caves, a narrow winding canyon carved into sinuous curves by water. Then climb up an enormous sand dune and peer over cliffs that appear like sloping bookshelves. Marvel at the moonlike expanse of reddish sand far below, devoid of plant life, and the strange knobs and ridges of rock that look as if they could have been cast in a *Star Wars* movie.

OPPOSITE: **A lone hiker makes his way through the Devil's Gorge near San Pedro de Atacama.**

NEXT PAGES: **Take in panoramic views of Valle de la Luna from Achaches lookout.**

"I was so astounded and taken aback," says Macca Sherifi, a U.K.-based travel blogger, photographer, and founder of the website AnAdventurousWorld.com. "It's this alien landscape. They call it the Valley of the Moon, but it could almost be Mars with the color of the rock and how red and dusty brown it is. It's one of the most beautiful places I've been."

Sunset is a particularly great time to experience this place. Overhead, the sky is usually a gargantuan dome of blue or a theater where clouds play out their melodramas. Watch as their shadows travel across the land and the sun illuminates different parts of the cliffs. Feel the temperature drop as the sun descends, and be still as the dwindling light paints the stone saturated tones of red, orange, and pink. Night in the desert might turn chilly, but it can also be magical when stars start poking through the navy twilight.

KNOW BEFORE YOU GO

Because the Atacama Desert is so high, the temperatures aren't as broiling as one might expect in a desert at a similar latitude, hovering in the 70s Fahrenheit (20s Celsius) during the day and the high 30s and 40s Fahrenheit (around 0°C and the single digits Celsius) at night. It's also wise to drink plenty of water and electrolytes to stay hydrated in the face of altitude sickness.

AUYANTEPUI MOUNTAIN

To the Edge of the Abyss

DISTANCE: Varies   **LENGTH OF TRIP: 9 days**
BEST TIME TO GO: December through April   **DIFFICULTY: Strenuous**

Among the sandstone tabletop mountains of Venezuela, known as *tepuis*, Auyantepui stands as the largest. An imposing massif, it looms over verdant valleys, often ensconced in mists. A trek up this fearsome mountain affords a singular view of these unusual formations as well as the mountaintop's unique geology and endemic flora.

The trek to the top generally takes about three days and is best suited to highly experienced hikers. Hiring a guide is mandatory. From the Kamarata Valley, which can be reached by plane from Bolivar, stay in a welcoming Pémon community, and hike up through savannas. Walk through forest festooned in flowers, bromeliads, and vines, then scramble up a steep, slippery notch in the tepui with the help of ropes.

"I have been going there for 25 years and for me it's a very special place," says Esteban Torbar, the president of Eposak, a foundation that promotes sustainable tourism in the valley. "It's like a completely different planet—this mountain is 700 square kilometers [270 sq mi] and there's only one path to get to the top." Behold an Eden of pink-sand beaches, waterfalls, rivers tinted orange by tannins, and strange fields of thumblike rock formations. Hikers spend several days exploring these wonders before heading back down the lush cliff face.

WHAT YOU'LL SEE: Flowers | Bromeliads | Vines | Pink-sand beaches | Waterfalls

HISTORICAL FOOTNOTE

Non-natives first spotted Angel Falls, which tumbles 3,212 feet (980 m) off the face of Auyantepui, in the 1930s. The waterfall was subsequently named for James Angel, an American daredevil pilot who crashed his plane nearby in 1937. But in 2009, President Hugo Chávez declared that it should be called by the indigenous name, Kerepakupai Ven.

Angel Falls, the world's highest waterfall, tumbles more than 2,600 feet (800 m) from the top of Mount Auyantepui.

ARA O TE MOAI

On the Path of the Ancients in Easter Island

DISTANCE: 1.2 miles (2 km) point to point **LENGTH OF TRIP:** 1 hour
BEST TIME TO GO: Year-round **DIFFICULTY:** Easy

Known as Rapa Nui to its original inhabitants, Easter Island is 2,200 miles (3,500 km) off the coast of Chile, making it one of the most remote inhabited islands in the world. Picture empty beaches, turbulent waters, and night skies unmarred by even a hint of urban light pollution. Made of extinct volcanoes and hardened lava fields, this isle is renowned for its *moai,* or gigantic stone statues, and shrines, which were fashioned by indigenous residents largely between the 1300s and 1600s. Hundreds of statues remain and, along with other archaeological sites, attract visitors from around the world.

Many trails thread through open, desolate hills, which offer uninterrupted vistas, beckoning to both walkers and horseback riders. One thought-provoking hike is Ara O Te Moai, which follows a transport route that the ancients used to move the stone statues from a quarry near the volcanic crater to their resting places around the island. From west to east, hikers travel along this easy trail with spectacular views of the ocean. More and more fallen moai dot the trail as you get closer to the quarry where the ancients carved these monolithic sculptures.

"It's like being in a movie," says Marcus Edensky, founder of Easter Island Travel, which guides hikers and offers tours around the island. "People made these statues with their own hands out of rock, and you get to walk about the remnants of the past. It's all for real, it's not made up—you really feel that here."

WHAT YOU'LL SEE: *Moai* statues I Free-roaming horses I *Moko uri uri* lizards

ALTERNATIVE ROUTE

For avid hikers who'd prefer more miles under their feet, try the North Coast hike, which covers 13 miles (21 km) point to point through a remote roadless area between a volcano and the sea on the island's northern tip. It's best to hire a guide who can point out archaeological ruins and fallen statues as you travel along seaside cliffs.

Hundreds of Easter Island's famous, mystical *moai* pepper the Ara O Te Moai trail, dazzling walkers.

COTOPAXI VOLCANO

The Sleeping Giant

DISTANCE: 9 miles (15 km) out and back   **LENGTH OF TRIP:** 3-plus days
BEST TIME TO GO: Year-round   **DIFFICULTY:** Expert-only

The perfect cone of Cotopaxi—one of the tallest volcanoes in the world at 19,345 feet (5,896 m)—reigns over Ecuador's central highlands like an imperious monarch, all but taunting climbers to brave her slopes. Situated in a string of volcanoes in the Cordillera Central of the Andes, it has been known for spectacular eruptions. But when this towering giant naps, climbers flock here because few volcanoes this tall are so easily accessible.

Those who attempt this peak should have experience with an ice ax, crampons, and glacier travel (yes, its peak is covered in snow and ice), but the route is typically suitable for intermediate climbers. The biggest challenge is the altitude itself. "It's a whole different world up there," says Michael Walter, a mountain guide with RMI Expeditions, who has climbed Cotopaxi more than two dozen times. "Everything gets harder because of the lack of oxygen. You climb a lot slower. Your heart is pumping and your lungs are burning." If altitude sickness sets in, climbers might have a headache, feel nauseous, or lose their appetite.

In order to acclimate to the high altitude on expeditions up the peak, visitors generally spend a few days in Quito and the surrounding countryside, then base their summit bid out of the Jose Ribas Refugio. A well-kept hut often packed with mountain climbers, it sits at nearly 16,000 feet (4,900 m)

OPPOSITE: Standing 19,393 feet (5,911 m), Cotopaxi is one of Ecuador's most active volcanoes, erupting more than 50 times since the 16th century.

NEXT PAGES: Donning crampons, climbers take on the glacier peak of Cotopaxi.

but is only a casual hike from the nearest road. On summit day, alpinists wake up at midnight and set off climbing with only the narrow beam of a head-lamp to light the way. The smell of sulfur from the volcano's inner workings sporadically wafts through the air. Listen to the crunch of crampons on hardened snow as you ascend the 30- to 50-degree slopes of the volcano's crevasse-lined glaciers. The route leads more than 3,000 vertical feet (about 1,000 m) up but never becomes more technical than a steep walk.

After negotiating the summit ramp, climbers usually top out at about six or seven in the morning. From the summit, peer down into the dark volcanic crater made of rock and ice. If it's clear, cottony clouds stretch below with only the peaks of other volcanoes poking through. If you're especially lucky and the skies are gin clear, you can see all the way down to the forests and patchwork farmland far below.

KNOW BEFORE YOU GO

Climbers tackling Cotopaxi should have some prior mountaineering experience. "We recommend that people climb Mount Rainier before Cotopaxi because it's a very good test," says mountain guide Michael Walter. "It's very similar terrain, you're using the exact same equipment, and it's similar temperatures. You just add the variable of altitude on Cotopaxi."

SANTA LUCIA CLOUD FOREST

Life in a Land of Shifting Fog

DISTANCE: About 3 miles (5 km) out and back   **LENGTH OF TRIP: 2 hours**
BEST TIME TO GO: October through May   **DIFFICULTY: Moderate**

Cloud forests are persnickety about where they grow—only in the high elevations of tropical mountain ranges, where rain is heavy and condensation bejewels the plants thanks to warm, moist air that rises into the peaks. These woodlands, also known as montane rainforests, see many threats, such as agriculture and pollution, but climate change could be the biggest, as temperatures warm and cool-loving forests are pushed up and off the mountainsides.

Experience one of these unique forests by visiting a forward-thinking Ecuadorian community that committed its land to conservation and eco-tourism instead of agriculture. The resulting preserve, Santa Lucia, may be small at 1,804 acres (730 ha), but it is more than 80 percent virgin rainforest and attracts scientists and students from all over the world. They typically stay in the community-run, electricity-free, eponymous ecolodge that sits atop a lush mountain only reachable by a 1.5-mile (2.5-km) footpath. Hiking here is not necessarily about big splashy views—although the vistas over the hills wrapped in mists aren't shabby—but rather immersing oneself in the life of the forest, which requires a keen eye and mindful patience.

Six trails traverse the reserve, including one rumored to be an ancient pre-Inca trade route. One standout is the three-mile (5-km) round-trip Waterfall Trail, which leads down off the hillside, plunging through rainforest to three

OPPOSITE: A lucky sight in the forest, a spectacled bear climbs a tree in search of fruit.

NEXT PAGES: Santa Lucia Reserve is 1,804 acres (730 ha) of virgin rainforest promoting eco-tourism and conservation.

WHAT YOU'LL SEE:

Waterfalls | Orchids | Hummingbirds |
Morpho butterflies | Agoutis | Lowland
pacas | Spectacled bears | Mountain tanagers |
Cocks-of-the-rock | Mountain toucans

cascades and finally down to the Santa Rosa River with pools of cool water almost demanding to be swum. Take your time marching down the sometimes-muddy slopes. There's much to be seen: Delicate orchids languidly sprawl in the understory. Hummingbirds buzz by. Magnificent iridescent blue morpho butterflies drift alongside you.

In parts of these forests, agoutis and lowland pacas—spotted guinea pig–like mammals—join snakes and frogs in the underbrush. The spectacled bear is a resident in this region, too. But the birds, of course, always steal the spotlight. It's not uncommon for birders to see upwards of 70 species over the course of a few days in this cloud forest. Keep an eye out for species like the blue-winged mountain tanager, cock-of-the-rock, and plate-billed mountain toucan. And if you don't spot them, let your ears be your guide, opened to the wild hoots and chirps and tweets of this high mountain forest.

WILDLIFE SPOTTING

The spectacled bear, also known as the Andean bear, is the only bear species in South America and is named for its light-colored markings around the eyes. Very shy and solitary, these animals make their homes high in the cloud forests and subsist mostly on fruit and other plants as well as some birds, insects, and rodents.

CIUDAD PERDIDA TREK

An Indiana Jones–Style Jungle Adventure

DISTANCE: 29 miles (47 km) out and back   **LENGTH OF TRIP:** 4 to 5 days
BEST TIME TO GO: December through March   **DIFFICULTY:** Strenuous

D eep in the Sierra Nevada de Santa Marta in northern Colombia, the remains of an ancient city known as Ciudad Perdida (the Lost City), or Teyuna, hide high in the Buritaca River Basin between about 3,000 and 4,000 feet (900–1,200 m). Indigenous people inhabited this city from about the sixth century to the 16th century A.D., and presumably abandoned it when the Spanish stormed through. Local people, who claim to be descendants of the original inhabitants, say they have known about it for centuries; in 1976, outside archaeologists started carrying out excavations, and it soon became known to the world.

Today, a rugged trail leads to these beautiful stone ruins, often likened to a wilder version of Machu Picchu and unique in the country. Although thousands of intrepid travelers tackle the 29-mile (47-km) round-trip trek annually, it's far from a breeze. The ascents require a good degree of fitness, and the hair-raising descents demand sturdy joints. The heat and humidity also add another degree of challenge, although evenings can be cool if the wind picks up. Think of the experience as a muddy, bug-infested, Indiana Jones–style sweat-fest.

Trekkers travel through open, treeless areas that were once used as agricultural land, then plunge into deep jungle and tunnels of leafy, vine-choked greenery. Several times, hikers must wade through the Buritaca River—often

OPPOSITE: La Ciudad Perdida was built about 650 years before Machu Picchu and is accessible only by foot.

NEXT PAGES: Vine- and moss-covered steps in an old-growth forest lead to the Lost City.

the water is knee-high or even reaches your chest. (Many hikers choose to travel during the dry season, December through March, to avoid high river crossings.) Ascents and descents can be steep, and it rains frequently, turning sections of trail into a mucky mess. And it's best not to be too squeamish about creepy crawlies; this lush, vibrant jungle is full of spiders, ants, snakes, and frogs. Trekkers typically stay in rustic designated camps along the trail, which offer bunks and hammocks—and, on occasion, beautiful clear swimming holes to wash the day's hike away.

The final challenge before reaching this ancient city is some 1,200 small, moss-slicked stone steps etched into a hillside. (Keep your hands free.) Take time to amble through these high terraces and stone walls framed by palms and ogle the views over the hills beyond. What would it have been like to dwell in this well-organized city among these forests a millennium ago?

KNOW BEFORE YOU GO

Archaeological sites are fragile and irreplaceable. As many as 130 people visit Ciudad Perdida every day. While soldiers guard it and archaeologists perform preservation work, it's best to watch your step, avoid walking on walls or moving rocks, and leave everything as you found it for the next visitors.

CASCADA FIN DEL MUNDO

A Watery Amazonian Paradise

DISTANCE: 3.4 miles (5.5 km) out and back **LENGTH OF TRIP:** 3 hours
BEST TIME TO GO: December through March **DIFFICULTY:** Easy

There's no reason to rush to the end of the world—Fin del Mundo—a 246-foot (75-m) waterfall hidden in the jungle just south of Mocoa in Putumayo, a southwestern region of Colombia. The journey through this Amazonian forest is just as delightful as the payoff. From the trailhead, where a small fee is requested from the land's private owners, hikers travel through rainforest covered in moss and packed with ferns, vines, and heliconias to the Dantayaco River. Weaving along the banks, the trail visits a series of rushing cascades and shimmering pools that, in the dry months between August and March, glow a clear, inviting emerald green.

The weather is often hot and muggy and the trail can be muddy, which means swim breaks are irresistible. Popular among visitors as well as locals, part of the fun of this trail is the socializing—visitors loll in the water and laze on the banks as if frolicking in some unknown Eden. Move slowly to spot some of the forest's denizens, including colorful birds, exotic insects, and monkeys. Finally, you'll make it to the waterfall itself, which free-falls into yet another swimming pool. Some visitors even clamber to the top and rappel down into the pool below.

WHAT YOU'LL SEE: Amazon forest | Ferns | Heliconias | Dantayaco River | Waterfalls | Pools | Monkeys | Exotic insects

ALTERNATIVE ROUTE

The same trailhead also offers access to another natural attraction via about a half-hour walk: Ojo de Dios ("Eye of God"), a waterfall cascading through a hole in an overhanging rock. At certain times of day, the light streams in like a spotlight, illuminating the water with an ethereal glow.

Hikers can crawl on their belly to the edge of the top of Fin del Mundo, a vertigo-inducing view of the falls tumbling into a pool below.

LAGUNA TORRE

A Glacial Lake and Its Towers

DISTANCE: 11 miles (18 km) out and back   **LENGTH OF TRIP:** 5 to 7 hours
BEST TIME TO GO: Austral spring through fall   **DIFFICULTY:** Moderate

From the high Andean climber's base camp of El Chalten, hikers can wander straight into the mountains of Los Glaciares National Park, a UNESCO World Heritage site, packed with glaciers steamrolling out of the gargantuan Southern Patagonia Ice Field. Granite peaks top out at more than 10,000 feet (3,000 m) high in this bastion of wildness. Even on a day hike, the weather conditions can inspire both fear and awe. On the flip side, even a day hike can yield views of some of the most renowned mountainscapes on Earth.

One of the most popular hikes in the park is accessible from footpaths that lead right from the outskirts of El Chalten: Laguna Torre. In just the first 15 minutes, you'll get views into the gorge of the Río Fitz Roy and a vista up the valley and into the Adela Range. Over about five-and-a-half miles (9 km), you'll walk along the river, through southern beech forests and big open plains, until a field of boulders emerges. On top of a glacial moraine, find the Laguna Torre, a blue glacial lagoon flanked by peaks, including the soaring buttresses of the Fitz Roy Massif and famed Cerro Torre, a fickle objective that climbers have been attempting (and occasionally summiting) for decades. Stay for a while to contemplate its imposing vertical walls and the glacier across the lagoon that, along with other monumental ice sheets, seems responsible for this otherworldly landscape.

WHAT YOU'LL SEE: Río Fitz Roy | Adela Range | Beech forests | Laguna Torre glacial lagoon | Wildflowers

WILDLIFE SPOTTING

The Andean condor is a massive bird that hikers can spot coasting on thermals high above Patagonia's windy expanses. A relative of the vulture, condors are typically looking out for carcasses to clean up. These massive birds can grow wingspans of some 10 feet (3 m) in width, and the males have a telltale white collar around their necks.

On the way to glacial Laguna Torre, hikers have views of the Adela Range's rocky snow-covered peaks.

VALLE DE COCORA

A Forest of Slender Giants

DISTANCE: 7.7 miles (12.4 km) in a loop   **LENGTH OF TRIP:** 4 to 6 hours
BEST TIME TO GO: July through September   **DIFFICULTY:** Moderate

The iconic wax palms of Colombia have had a rough century or two. For years, farmers cleared the forests where they live to make way for plantations. Churchgoers plucked fronds from baby trees for Palm Sundays, and others collected the waxy coating from their trunks to make candles. Luckily, in 1985, the Colombian government established protections for these endangered giants, the highest palms in the world at about 200 feet (60 m) tall and the official national tree. Colombians are proud of these beautiful, charismatic giants. Now, one of the best places to see them is the Valle de Cocora in the coffee-growing region of Quindío.

From Salento, an attractive Andean backpacker's haven west of Bogotá, travelers hop on a four-wheel-drive vehicle for a 30-minute ride through lush countryside dotted with coffee and avocado plantations, to the Valle de Cocora. Some hikers stroll shorter out-and-back routes on a series of trails in the valley, many of which traverse private land, but the full five-hour loop allows for the best views and an immersion in the landscape. (From this valley, hikers can also access the high lakes and volcanoes of Los Nevados National Natural Park.)

Starting at a trailhead at nearly 7,000 feet (2,100 m), travel through high-altitude Andean forests packed with birds—keep an eye out for black-billed and great-breasted mountain toucans, the magnificent Andean condor, the

OPPOSITE: **Verdant Cocora Valley, just outside Salento, Colombia, is home to a cloud forest, lush jungle, and working farmland.**

NEXT PAGES: **The trek through the valley includes jungle and old-growth forest walks.**

WHAT YOU'LL SEE: Andean forests I Black-billed and great-breasted mountain toucans I Andean condors I Masked trogons I Sword-billed hummingbirds I Agoutis I Coatis I Cloud forests

colorful masked trogon, and the sword-billed hummingbird, which sports an unbelievably long beak. Agoutis, coatis, and other mammals also frequent these cloud forests, known for their moody shifting mists.

A good, lung-busting huff leads up to nearly 9,000 feet (2,700 m) where locals at La Finca la Montaña, a farmstead, share drinks. At this altitude, the temperature can dip into the 50s Fahrenheit (10+°C) so be sure to bring a few extra layers. From there, the rocky and sometimes muddy trail dips down and follows the river to a lookout point over the prize attraction: Stands of tall, slim palms sprout out of ultragreen pastures as if planted by some unseen hand. (Typically, the trees grow in forests and appear as a second canopy, but these individuals stand in open pastures after farmers cleared the rest of the land.) Marvel at the unusual Dr. Seuss–like landscape, created by a mix of natural and human forces.

POST-HIKE ACTIVITY

Coffee is a common crop in Quindío and well worth sampling. Local guides like Living Trips offer visits at coffee plantations on the way to hike the Valle de Cocora. Alternatively, in Salento, stop at Café Jesus Martín, which offers a range of coffees from around Colombia—and an enticing selection of delicious *tortas*.

THE PATI VALLEY

A Fantasyland of Tabletop Plateaus

DISTANCE: 39 miles (63 km) point to point   **LENGTH OF TRIP:** 4-plus days
BEST TIME TO GO: Austral winter and spring   **DIFFICULTY:** Moderate to strenuous

The vistas in Chapada Diamantina National Park are straight out of a fantasy movie: Table-shaped plateaus with sheer cliffs loom over wide valleys carpeted in unbroken green. Electric-blue swimming holes beckon to the weary and remote caves hide bizarre rock formations and serene pools.

In the state of Bahia in northeastern Brazil, this park is a hiker's paradise, and the Pati Valley, located in the Chapada Diamantina's northern half, is considered the most beautiful of all.

A former coffee-growing region, the Pati Valley has a network of trails, and local guides offer hiking trips ranging in length from a day to a week. The outfitter Diamantina Mountains, for example, offers a four-day, 39-mile (62-km) trip that leads up and down hillsides—sometimes slippery with mud—to mesas and vistas like Mirante do Pati, which overlooks a beautiful green cleft framed by rocky slopes.

Along the way keep an eye out for wildlife like parrots and coatis (small, cute raccoon relatives with striped trails), and stop at waterfalls to loll about in sparkling water and stare up at the sky.

In the evenings, hikers typically stay in the homes of locals, who offer meals made with regional ingredients like green papaya, bananas, manioc, and sweet potatoes. Hosts often share legends and tall tales well into the night.

WHAT YOU'LL SEE: Parrots I Coatis I Waterfalls I Amaryllis I Hummingbirds I Chaco eagles I White-necked hawks I Bahia spinetails I Giant armadillos

CULTURAL HIGHLIGHT

Lençóis is a gateway to the national park and a former diamond-mining town in a region known for the industry. While it is now mainly used as a jumping-off point for excursions into Chapada Diamantina, take an evening to stroll around cobblestone streets and enjoy colorfully painted 19th-century facades, cafés, and hole-in-the-wall restaurants.

The sweeping Pati Valley lies between sandstone-colored table mountains, protected within Chapada Diamantina National Park.

SIERRA NEGRA AND VOLCAN CHICO

A Hidden Galápagos Wonder

DISTANCE: 10 miles (16 km) out and back **LENGTH OF TRIP:** 4 to 6 hours

BEST TIME TO GO: Winter and spring **DIFFICULTY:** Moderate

On the stage of the Galápagos Islands, the unique wildlife tends to steal the show. Giant tortoises amble about, oblivious to human onlookers, and blue-footed boobies whistle and honk. Marine iguanas paddle through the sea and sea lions frolic and lounge. But unbeknownst to many visitors, these dark-rock islands are show-stoppers in and of themselves.

Volcanic in origin, the archipelago, situated in the Pacific Ocean some 600 miles (1,000 km) west of continental Ecuador, features shield volcanoes, peaks, cliffs, and craters—hints of the mind-blowing forces that created these islands thousands of years ago. Isabela is the largest in the chain and hikers have an exceptional opportunity to see an enormous shield volcano up close. Sierra Negra features a rim that stretches for six miles (about 10 km), making it one of the largest volcanic craters in the world.

Sierra Negra is also still active. In June 2018, the volcano belched plumes of ash and streams of lava after an earthquake cracked open fissures. About 50 people evacuated the slopes, and local officials barred tourists from coming close for their own safety. The volcanic activity continued through August of 2018; by its conclusion lava flows covered a total area of 11.8 square miles (30.6 sq km). While parts of the hiking path opened up again, officials keep a tight watch on this fiery peak.

OPPOSITE: A Galápagos turtle can weigh up to 475 pounds (215 kg) and live more than 100 years.

NEXT PAGES: The Sierra Negra, on Isabela Island, is one of the most active volcanoes in the Galápagos.

When the area is open to visitors, hikers follow a lava-rock path up a moderate incline through low carpets of vegetation, sparse trees, cactus, and lots of ferns to access the crater rim. While you might spot the occasional bird, wildlife, in general, is scarce. This hike is all about the shape of the land itself. Within a few miles on the trail, the crater appears sprawling over the island like a giant's shallow soup bowl. Far below, dark, barren fields of lava-rock stretch across the caldera's floor like a landscape out of the pages of *Lord of the Rings*.

Most hikers continue their journey, traveling along the rim toward Volcan Chico. En route, the plant life surrenders to a lunar volcanic landscape of beige, crimson, and ocher rocks. Walk in this desolate landscape of fumaroles, low hills, and craggy outcroppings, and enjoy the views from the volcano over Isabela before retracing your steps back to the trailhead.

HISTORICAL FOOTNOTE

The bishop of Panama was the first to discover the Galápagos when his ship veered off course in 1535. Over the centuries, Spanish explorers, whalers, seal hunters, and pirates all frequented the archipelago, but British naturalist Charles Darwin, who visited in 1835, made it famous. The islands' unique endemic species inspired his influential theory of natural selection.

PART THREE
EUROPE

The sun sets behind Monte Pelmo and
Monte Civetta as hikers trek the Alta
Via 1 in the Italian Dolomites (page 172).

ARCTIC CIRCLE TRAIL

A Vast Northern Hinterland

DISTANCE: 102.5 miles (165 km) point to point   **LENGTH OF TRIP:** 7 to 12 days
BEST TIME TO GO: Summer and early fall   **DIFFICULTY:** Moderate

The few buildings of a scientific research station just outside of Kangerlussuaq, Greenland, are the last bits of civilization hikers see before embarking west on the Arctic Circle Trail (ACT). Leaving humanity behind, what strikes people most is the sheer immensity of the landscape. In all directions, low hills and plateaus stretch for what seems like an eternity, all topped by an enormous Arctic sky washed a periwinkle blue in midsummer.

"You feel an incredible sense of space," says Huw Thomas, a Welsh hiker who has visited the Arctic Circle Trail and the surrounding wilderness nine times since 2006 and advises other hikers. "But it can also feel a little bit daunting for some people. There's no stopping halfway and getting a bus back to town. Once you're committed, you either walk it or go back."

For most, Greenland is a blank spot on the map. An enormous island covered by an ice sheet as thick as two miles (3 km), it has relatively few inhabitants and, despite its name, very little green space. But human beings have flourished here for millennia.

In summer, in western Greenland, an ice-free swath of land is a repository of barren beauty. The Arctic Circle Trail starts from the settlement of Kangerlussuaq and runs 102.5 miles (165 km) to Sisimiut, a town on the western coast, going straight through this treeless tundra. Those with extra ambition

KNOW BEFORE YOU GO

Two things surprise hikers the most about the ACT: the mosquitoes and the warmth. If you go in midsummer, make sure to bring a couple of mesh head nets for the bugs. Also pack layers of clothing, since temperatures can range from near freezing at night to the upper 70s Fahrenheit (mid-20s Celsius) during the day.

OPPOSITE: Camping next to a glacier—in this case, the Russell Glacier—is a highlight of the Arctic Circle Trail.

NEXT PAGES: There are numerous river crossings along the trail.

tack on another 23 miles (37 km) at the beginning of the trek so that they can start at the Greenland Ice Sheet, which all but defines the country—at 660,234.7 square miles (1,710,000 sq km) it covers roughly 80 percent of the country's surface area—and its way of life.

Because of the Arctic Circle Trail's low elevation, the walking typically isn't difficult. Hikers follow a narrow two-boot-wide trail through bogs, marshes, deep spongy grass, and along ridgetops and hard, exposed rock. The landscape consists of wide plateaus, valleys, and pure clear lakes that sometimes stretch for 20 miles (32 km). The path is largely well marked with cairns, but losing it briefly can be disorienting—if you're in a thicket of dwarf shrub heath, birch, or willow, the trail could be a stone's throw away but remain invisible.

This wildness, of course, is a large part of the

CULTURAL HIGHLIGHT

The ACT passes through the Aasivissuit-Nipisat area, an Inuit hunting ground that was designated a UNESCO World Heritage site in 2018 for its 4,500-year-old cultural history. Archaeological sites from the Saqqaq, Dorset, and Thule Inuit people, as well as the colonial period, dot the land where people have been hunting caribou and fishing arctic char for millennia.

appeal. Visitors see reindeer antlers, bones, and periodically the majestic animals themselves. On occasion, families of musk ox will appear. Early in the season, arctic foxes trot about the land in their fluffy white fur coats, searching for arctic hares, only to stage a gradual costume change to brown later in the season. Birds are especially plentiful here. On the lakes, listen to the chilling calls of loons. Keep an eye out for gregarious long-tailed ducks, geese, eagles, and the red-necked phalarope, a delicate seabird that nests in pools of water in the tundra.

The skies are often benevolently clear in summertime, and many hikers camp along the way. There are also 10 rudimentary huts with bunks that dot the trail about a day's walk apart. (Get there early in case there are a lot of other hikers.) In these basic four walls, swap stories with other hikers and conk out to the sounds of the Arctic breezes.

GREAT ROUTE OF SÃO JORGE

A Lush Volcanic Citadel in the Atlantic

DISTANCE: 26 miles (42 km) point to point   **LENGTH OF TRIP: 2 days**
BEST TIME TO GO: Summer and fall   **DIFFICULTY: Moderate**

About 1,000 miles (1,600 km) off the coast of Portugal, nine volcanic islands rise out of the Atlantic Ocean like fortresses. Known as the Azores, they have made a haven for ocean-crossing sailors for centuries. But in recent years, the archipelago, a wild collection of craters, hot springs, fumaroles, deep forests, and rugged stone shores, has also gained fame as an off-the-beaten-track destination for nature seekers. Since 2014, locals have developed a series of great routes that traverse the islands so that visitors can immerse themselves in the rugged landscapes. Among the best is the Great Route of São Jorge.

The island of São Jorge sits in the middle of the archipelago and is renowned as a UNESCO World Biosphere Reserve, established in 2016 for the island's unique *fajãs,* or flat seaside peninsulas formed by collapsed cliffs or lava flows. Thanks to its dramatic topography from rocky seashore to high-altitude grasslands, São Jorge is also rife with endemic plants and animals. The Great Route traverses some 26 miles (42 km) of this unique terrain, from the eastern tip of the island along the southern shore to the north, in two stages. Since no wild camping is allowed, visitors typically stay in Fajã dos Vimes, a tiny hamlet of red-roofed homes on the southern coast.

Walk along high plateaus and among farms that have capitalized on this area's fertile land and warm, humid summer weather. (This island is home to

OPPOSITE: A traditional Azores chapel anchors a street in the town of Topo.

NEXT PAGES: The protected coastal fishing village of Fajã dos Cubres maintains the Hermitage of Our Lady of Lourdes, built in 1908, and protected flora and fauna.

WHAT YOU'LL SEE: Craters I Hot springs I Fumaroles I Forests I Waterfalls

Europe's only coffee plantation.) Stop for views over the cliffs, draped in magnificent and unusual-looking native plants, and for swims in waterfall pools and even the refreshing—some might say frigid—ocean. Just offshore, these waters teem with dolphins and whales. Since the island is in the middle of the archipelago, you can see various other islands as you travel northward. And as the sun moves between shifting clouds and fog, the light changes and the colors of the hills morph. What arguably strikes hikers the most, however, are the locals themselves.

"One thing that surprises a lot of people is the local people and the way we receive the tourists," says Luis Paulo Bettencourt, who was born on São Jorge and now guides hikers through his outdoor company Aventour. "People are very kind and friendly. You're hiking and someone invites you to come eat, drink wine, even stay with them. Here this is normal."

CULTURAL HIGHLIGHT

After a long day of walking, indulge in some of the Azores' excellent cuisine and local wines. Fish soup is a common dish across the islands, which depend on the abundance of the sea. And in São Jorge, sample a hearty local dish of yam, pork ribs, and two different types of sausage.

CAMINO DE SANTIAGO

Europe's Great Pilgrimage

DISTANCE: Camino Francés—nearly 500 miles (800 km) point to point   **LENGTH OF TRIP:** 30-plus days
BEST TIME TO GO: Summer and early fall   **DIFFICULTY:** Strenuous

The Camino de Santiago—or the Way of St. James—is much more than a hike. It's a pilgrimage. Those who set out on one of the dozens of routes to the tomb of St. James in Santiago de Compostela follow in the footsteps of millions who have undertaken similar journeys since the 12th century. (The earliest guidebook dates to the 1100s.) Those early pilgrims were determined to reach the tomb of the Apostle St. James, which was discovered in the early ninth century, as a sacred rite. Today, many walkers do it as a religious experience, while others undertake the journey seeking perspective and clarity during important junctures in their lives. No matter what the reasons for attempting the hike, it's hard to come away from "the way," as it's known to pilgrims, without being transformed.

For many, the most powerful part of the walk is the people. Hikers come from all over the planet and annually number in the hundreds of thousands. They often make fast friends with each other, and small talk and inhibitions tend to fall away within the first few miles as they form bonds over a shared purpose.

The challenges are plentiful. First, one must choose which route to walk from many that spiral outward into Spain, Portugal, and France. The most popular is the Camino Francés, which starts in Saint-Jean-Pied-de-Port in the

CULTURAL HIGHLIGHT

Even celebrities can't resist the allure of the Camino. In 2000, Shirley MacLaine wrote *The Camino: A Journey of the Spirit* **about her own experience on the route. And numerous movies have been filmed about and along it, including** *The Way,* **with Martin Sheen and Emilio Estevez, released in 2010.**

OPPOSITE: Walking sticks are sold with shells decorated with symbols of the Camino de Santiago.

NEXT PAGES: The beautiful Celtic O Cebreiro village is the first stop for pilgrims entering Galicia, Spain.

French Pyrénées. While the trail isn't exactly Himalayan in altitude or steepness, carrying one's belongings and walking 15-plus miles (25-plus km) a day on old roads over the course of a month or more can lead to exhaustion, numerous blisters, and screaming muscles. This, of course, is all part of the shared experience.

To make the most of the experience, preparation is key. While there isn't any technical walking, hikers should be fit enough to tromp for many hours. Because summertime is when most Europeans take vacations (and it can be desperately hot in Spain), the shoulder seasons of late spring and early fall are lovely times to set off.

Luckily, the scenery along the way is pleasantly rewarding. The Camino Francés, for example, crosses the northern Iberian Peninsula, passing through hilly pasturelands dotted with cows, medieval towns, forests ensconced in moss and mists, and blooming roadside flowers. You'll pass by ancient churches, stone buildings, and

KNOW BEFORE YOU GO

Before setting off on your journey, procure a *credencial,* or pilgrim's passport, and get it stamped at lodgings along the way. If you have a stamped *credencial,* have walked more than 62 miles (100 km) of the Camino, and declare a spiritual or religious intention, officials at the cathedral in Santiago will offer you an official certificate of pilgrimage.

ABOVE: Part of the pilgrimage route takes hikers past Cirauqui vineyards in Navarra, Spain.

OPPOSITE: The hike ends at the Cathedral of Santiago de Compostela, a World Heritage site and resting place for the tomb of St. James.

centuries-old bridges, and come to rest every evening in *albergues,* lodgings specifically meant for pilgrims. Restaurants also cater to walkers, offering discounted meals. And hikers are often surprised and grateful for the generosity offered along the trail.

While walking a dozen or more miles (20+ km) a day necessitates a steady pace, there's no need for haste. Savor the flavors of a meal offered in kindness by a local and shared with new friends. Linger over coffee with local grandpas turning the pages of a newspaper on a bright, cool morning. Listen to the sounds of the birds as a new day begins. And, finally, at the cathedral in Santiago, a beautiful Romanesque stone structure first started in 1075 and embellished and fortified over the centuries, take time to reflect on your journey among the great paintings, sculptures, and hushed murmurings of the hundreds of people who reached this spot alongside you.

SAMARIA GORGE

A Dramatic Canyon on Crete's Mesmerizing Coast

DISTANCE: 10 miles (16 km) point to point **LENGTH OF TRIP:** 4 to 6 hours
BEST TIME TO GO: Summer and early fall **DIFFICULTY:** Moderate

Crete's White Mountains are riddled with chasms but Samaria is the queen of them all. One of the longest canyons in Europe, this dramatic cleft snakes down from the goat-dotted highlands of Greece's biggest island to the small village of Agia Roumeli on its steep and spectacular southern shore. The 10-mile (16-km) downhill hike through this canyon is extremely popular but not easy. The first couple miles (3 km) are particularly steep, loose, and slippery, which means careful steps and good sturdy shoes are key. But the challenge is undoubtedly worth it.

As you walk down the gorge, pass through deep, shady pine forests and along the rocky shores of a stream, which tumbles into small cascades. Over time, the walls of the gorge soar as high as 1,000 feet (300 m) and narrow to as little as a few yards. You'll cross the river on stones and rickety wooden bridges countless times. Along the way, stop to take in sights like a Byzantine chapel, the ruins of an ancient village, the aquamarine pools of mountain water, and possibly the *kri kri*, the wild Cretan goat. Once you reach the sea, the best rewards await: a beer at a local café and a dip in the clear bathwater-warm Libyan Sea.

WHAT YOU'LL SEE: Pine forests I Streams I Small waterfalls I Byzantine chapel I Ancient village ruins I Cretan goats (*kri kri*)

KNOW BEFORE YOU GO

Most Samaria Gorge hikers start in the morning then catch the evening ferry to Sougia or Hora Sfakion. But very confident hikers might consider leaving later to have the gorge to themselves, then stay overnight in the village. The next day, relax on an empty beach, snorkel offshore, or stroll along an ancient coastal path to a Byzantine chapel.

The hike to the bottom of Europe's deepest canyon takes about four hours but is well worth the effort.

STROMBOLI VOLCANO

A Blazing Spectacle on the Aeolian Islands

DISTANCE: 6.2 miles (10 km) out and back   **LENGTH OF TRIP: 5 hours**
BEST TIME TO GO: Year-round   **DIFFICULTY: Moderate**

Most of the time, the fiery inner life of the earth is hidden from our view—with the notable exception of Stromboli. An ash-covered cone sticking out of Italy's Tyrrhenian Sea, it erupts almost constantly, sending spectacular plumes of hot magma as high as 1,200 feet (360 m) into the sky. Volcanologists estimate that the volcano has been erupting continuously for at least 3,000 years and probably many thousands more. Dubbed the "Lighthouse of the Mediterranean," it's visible from quite a distance. The reliable fireworks show and the crater's accessibility earn it a place among the most visited volcanoes on Earth.

One of a chain of picturesque islets off Sicily's northeast coast, Stromboli is easy to access by ferry or hydrofoil. Many visitors head out into the sea at night to see lava catapult out of the crater. But a hike to the summit of this island, clad in a skein of greenery and ringed by rocky shores and black-sand beaches, affords a much better view. Three trails lead up to the summit but the "new path" is the most popular.

About three hours before sunset, hikers start the 3,000-vertical-foot (900-m) climb, sweating up slopes covered in hardy shrubs, heather, small endemic flowers, and sweet-scented herbs. On the upper slopes, huff through sand and black ash to a perch overlooking the crater. From the top, views stretch

OPPOSITE: **Lava spurts and flows from Stromboli, which has had near-constant activity for at least 3,000 years.**

NEXT PAGES: **Hikers make their way up the northern slope of the volcano at sunset.**

WHAT YOU'LL SEE: An active volcanic crater |
Erupting lava | Black-sand beaches |
Shrubs | Heather | Herbs | Ash

over the other islands, the placid sea, and even to Mount Etna on Sicily, all cast with the warm glow of sunset.

Below, several vents sporadically spout steam, ash, rocks known as *lapilli,* and hot magma. Sulfur scents the air and, depending on the volcano's mood, eruptions occur between every two minutes and every two hours to a chorus of oohs and ahs from mesmerized hikers.

"To see the faces of the people when they go up, it's a real reward," says Lorenzo Russo, a hiking guide who founded the local outfitter Magmatrek more than 20 years ago. "They put their hands on their mouths and open their eyes wide. Sometimes they cry. Sometimes they even get scared, but always this reaction of wonder, of surprise."

On the descent, under the cover of darkness, skid down the ash like snow all the way to the town of Stromboli, where you can fall into bed in a local *albergo,* perhaps dreaming about the mysterious inner workings of the planet's blazing core.

HISTORICAL FOOTNOTE

The Aeolian Islands—*Isole Eolie* in Italian—were named a UNESCO World Heritage site in 2000 because of their rich history in the scientific study of volcanism. Starting in the 1700s, and perhaps earlier, volcano buffs have come here to study two types of eruption: Strombolian and Vulcanian.

ITALY

THE CINQUE TERRE

Cliffs, Colorful Villages, and the Sparkling Sea

DISTANCE: 9 miles (14.5 km) point to point   **LENGTH OF TRIP: 1 to 3 days**
BEST TIME TO GO: Spring and fall   **DIFFICULTY: Moderate**

On the Italian Riviera, on the northwest coast of Italy, five villages cling to seaside cliffs. Known as Cinque Terre, or five lands, they're a fairy-tale-like vision of pastel-hued homes, immaculate churches, narrow lanes, and beaches dotted with rows of umbrellas and bathers in colorful attire. The towns are linked by boat and train, but the best way to see them is on foot via a network of narrow cliff-skimming footpaths that offer spectacular views of the Ligurian Sea and the rocky slopes that plunge into it.

On your way between Monterosso al Mare in the north and Riomaggiore in the south (or vice versa), travel through picturesque lemon orchards, olive groves, and stands of chestnut trees as you meander up and down over a day or two. Some hikers take their time and stay in small village hotels along the route. Even on a day hike there's no need to rush, as delightful distractions beckon at every turn: Amble around a 15th-century castle in Riomaggiore, breaststroke through turquoise waters offshore, visit terraced vineyards, and, of course, stop for fresh gelato, cappuccino, and long languid lunches of fresh fish and *vino* along the way.

**WHAT YOU'LL SEE: Colorful cliffside homes I Beaches I Ligurian Sea I
Lemon orchards I Olive groves I Vineyards I Chestnut trees**

KNOW BEFORE YOU GO

Like many of the world's exceptionally beautiful destinations, Cinque Terre suffers from too much love—so much so that local officials introduced a service card system to limit the impact of visitors in the villages. (Proceeds help maintain and restore the territory and provide transportation to visitors.) Consider visiting in the spring and fall, when the number of tourists ebbs.

Part of the trail through Cinque Terre National Park passes a church and vineyard in Manarola village.

ALTA VIA DELLE DOLOMITI 1

A High Route Through the Heart of the Dolomites

DISTANCE: 78 miles (125 km) point to point **LENGTH OF TRIP:** 8 to 12 days
BEST TIME TO GO: Summer **DIFFICULTY:** Strenuous

The Alta Via 1, a long-distance footpath through northern Italy's Dolomite Mountains, starts off with a bang. In a steep-sloped valley carpeted with evergreens, the surreal turquoise Lago di Bràies perfectly reflects the mountains that rise from the lakeshore like intimidating gatekeepers—a tantalizing clue to the geological marvels to come.

The Alta Via—literally "high route"—is a series of existing trails first strung together as a high mountain traverse in the 1960s with the publication of a small guidebook, *Alta Via delle Dolomiti*. Hikers now take numerous variations from the original route, but the most common path winds from Lago di Bràies nearly 80 miles (125 km) all the way to Belluno, a small historic city full of Renaissance architecture.

Known for its light-gray dolomitic limestone, this unusual mountain range is chock-full of strange shapes, pinnacles, fins, serrated ridges, plunging gorges, and huge slopes of scree, created over centuries by erosion. To say the terrain is rugged would be an understatement. Hikers on the Alta Via 1 commonly encounter tough ascents, only to be followed by a knee-busting descent and yet another mind-fraying climb. Changes in weather or unexpected snowfall can happen at any time.

But while the walking is strenuous—some stages of the route climb more than 3,000 vertical feet (900 m) in a day—the paths are generally well-trod

WILDLIFE SPOTTING

Squirrels, deer, grouse, and eagles are a few of the more common species hikers spot in the Dolomites, but keep an eye out for the more elusive chamois, a small, goatlike mammal that lives in herds in the high mountains and sports striking black-and-white face markings and short, curved horns.

OPPOSITE: The Croda da Lago refuge is perched on peaceful Lake Federa.

NEXT PAGES: Alta Via 1 passes through the Passo Giau and Forcella Ambrizzola area, in the shadow of Mount Pelmo.

and, conveniently, the Italians have built *rifugios* a day's walk apart the entire way, making this trek an immersion in extremes, from the wildness of the surroundings to the relative comfort of the *rifugios*. (A word to the wise: Book your bunks far in advance and bring earplugs.)

Some ambitious hikers veer off into even more challenging terrain, like scrambles up the peaks or *vie ferrate,* routes established during World War I with rungs and cables to help soldiers navigate highly exposed terrain. (Between 1915 and 1918, soldiers also built posts, trenches, barracks, and tunnels through the mountains, braving avalanches and extreme cold.) Today, vie ferrate are commonly used by recreationists to access airy nooks of the mountains—and supreme views. But one need not travel these high paths for a grand introduction to the Dolomites' legendary mountain scenery. Photographable vistas pop out at seemingly every turn—from the imposing

CULTURAL HIGHLIGHT

This region has always straddled the Latin and Germanic spheres and, as a result, there is a colorful mix of local languages. In addition to German and Italian, an estimated 50,000 locals also speak Ladin, an ancient regional romance language related to Romansch. Depending on the valley, *bun dé* or *bon dì* means "good day."

Lagazuoi Massif and the five fingers of the Cinque Torri to tiny alpine lakes and moonlike valleys. On a more intimate scale, the Dolomites are also known as a European hot spot for wildflowers, from the prized lady slipper orchid to purple lupines and orange lilies.

In the evenings, trekkers devour hearty meals in catered huts like Rifugio Lagazuoi (open summer and winter) or Rifugio Coldai (open June through September) among an international crowd. After a glass of wine (or two) wander out to gaze up at dark star-studded skies. Luckily, these hut builders had an uncanny knack for finding tremendously scenic spots—they are often perched on a mountain or cliff, or settled in a sea of peacefully undulating hills. Wake up early, not only to get a good start to the day but also to see the views from the *rifugios* as the rising sun paints the serrated peaks in tones of purple, peach, and pink.

TOUR DU MONT BLANC

Three Countries, One Alpine Wonderland

DISTANCE: 105 miles (168 km) in a loop **LENGTH OF TRIP:** 9 to 12 days
BEST TIME TO GO: Summer and early fall **DIFFICULTY:** Strenuous

Mont Blanc, the highest peak in western Europe at 15,781 feet (4,810 m), has inspired fear and ambition in European climbers for centuries. Its massif sprawls over France, Italy, and Switzerland, forming a fortress of giant peaks and some of Europe's largest glaciers. This is the birthplace of modern mountaineering, where women and men have tested their nerve on high alpine routes since the 1700s. While the highest slopes demand climbing expertise, the alpine meadows form a walker's paradise, which is why the 105-mile (168-km) circumnavigation of the Mont Blanc Massif has become one of Europe's most popular hiking routes.

Many trekkers start in Chamonix, a mecca for mountaineers in summer and skiers in winter that sits in the shadow of Mont Blanc, which is muffled in snow for much of the year. Part of the great appeal of this trek is its juxtaposition of surreal, wild scenery and the delightful luxuries of civilization, from the occasional cable-car ride up a steep mountain to the welcoming accommodations and restaurants that dot the route. Each valley has its own architecture, traditions, and local foods. Hikers choose from staying in luxurious lodgings in tony resort towns like Courmayeur or in more basic catered huts high up in the mountains where they partake in rich evening meals soaked with local wine and *fromage*.

OPPOSITE: Locally made cheeses are for sale at the Saturday market in Chamonix, a great place to stop along the route.

NEXT PAGES: Mont Blanc dominates the skyline over the Val Vény, outside of the town of Courmayeur, Italy.

WHAT YOU'LL SEE: Three countries I Alpine meadows I **Wildflowers** I **Ancient Roman roads** I **Renaissance chapel** I **Glaciers**

The route, which passes from France into Italy and Switzerland, is also no joke. Hikers routinely climb more than 2,000 vertical feet (600 m) in a day and sometimes more than 4,000 (1,200 m). Some sections dare hikers with a measure of dizzying exposure. And the trail can be surprisingly steep. Then again, so is the scenery, which is the main draw. You'll all but have to stifle your urge to sing *Sound of Music* tunes as you pass through spectacular wildflower-flecked alpine meadows, ringed with jagged peaks. Along the way, hikers pass quintessentially European bits of history, from an ancient Roman road to a chapel with Renaissance frescoes. At the Mer de Glace, an iconic tourist attraction for at least a century and a half, ogle one of Europe's biggest glaciers, a behemoth of blue and white ice. And, naturally, the views of Mont Blanc, which emerges on crystalline blue-sky days, dazzle at every turn.

POST-HIKE ACTIVITY

You've earned your views. Now it's time to embrace the easy way up on the Téléphérique Aiguille du Midi, Europe's highest cable car. From Chamonix, this stomach-dropping 20-minute ride takes you straight up to 12,605 feet (3,842 m) where the Mont Blanc Range unfolds in all her glory, from the queen mountain herself to Monte Rosa and the Grand Combin.

ALETSCH PANORAMAWEG

Switzerland's Grandest Glacier Views

DISTANCE: 9.3 miles (15 km) point to point   **LENGTH OF TRIP:** 4 to 5 hours
BEST TIME TO GO: Midsummer to early fall   **DIFFICULTY:** Moderate

It's not hard to imagine why UNESCO designated the Swiss Alps Jungfrau-Aletsch region of Switzerland a World Heritage site: The most glaciated region of the Alps, it harbors a huge diversity of ecosystems and the Great Aletsch Glacier, the largest of its kind in Eurasia. In simpler terms, the mountain scenery will knock your socks off. And the Aletsch Panoramaweg, or panoramic trail, leads hikers straight into the heart of it.

The journey starts with a pleasant gondola ride up to the Bettmerhorn station, where the mountain trail starts off with immediate views of the gigantic ribbon of black-flecked ice known as the Great Aletsch. As you descend the rocky path through low vegetation and flowers, watch as the monster of ice slowly gets closer and closer.

After a couple of hours of hiking, the sparkling Märjelensee, a lake filled with glacial meltwater, comes into view and, soon after, there's the Gletscherstube, a simple wooden restaurant that serves typical Swiss dishes like hearty soups and *kaseschnitte,* bread baked with cheese and ham and topped with an egg. Linger over a glass of Valais wine before heading down to Fiescheralp, a small collection of vacation lodgings, with another handy cable car to whisk you down to the valley.

WHAT YOU'LL SEE: Glaciers | Märjelensee | Cable cars | Massa Gorge

THE CHALLENGE

You don't need to be an expert climber to cross the Great Aletsch Glacier. You just need crampons, some basic know-how, and a guide service. The outfitter Bergsteigerzentrum Aletsch, for example, offers two-day guided trips that take hikers from Jungfraujoch to the Konkordia Hut, then across the glacier in the gentle light of morning to Märjelensee, a small tranquil lake.

Trekkers use ice ridges to walk across the Swiss Aletsch Glacier, one of the largest ice streams in Europe.

SWISS WINE ROUTE

A World of Wine on the Swiss Riviera

DISTANCE: 7.3 miles (11.7 km) point to point **LENGTH OF TRIP:** 3 to 4 hours
BEST TIME TO GO: Spring, summer, and fall **DIFFICULTY:** Easy

Oenophiles have been growing wine grapes on the steep, south-facing shores of Lake Geneva since at least the 11th century and possibly as far back as Roman times. The result is a landscape renowned for its white *Chasselas* wines, which are still in production today, and marked by thousands of picturesque terraces.

Increasingly, the region is also known for another activity: walking. A delightful, mellow route wends along roads and pedestrian-only footpaths from St. Saphorin, a medieval village of slim cobbled lanes and centuries-old homes, to Lutry, a lively medieval city along Lake Geneva with boutiques and cafés. Between the two, walkers amble between teeny villages and orderly lines of vineyards with views of the navy-blue lake and the Alps beyond. With scheduled appointments, you can stop at vineyards, or simply wander into wine bars like Lavaux Vinorama in Rivaz, which showcases nearly 300 wines from the region—and will let you taste quite a few of them in its attractive contemporary tasting room.

Rest assured that after all of that walking and wine tasting, the Swiss have thought of everything, including a punctual scenic train that whisks hikers back to their evening abodes.

WHAT YOU'LL SEE: Lake Geneva I Medieval villages I Vineyards and wineries I Wine bars

POST-HIKE ACTIVITY

Every village along this route boasts its own beach, generally made of small, gray stones. Some swimming areas even have cloakrooms and showers for changing. On a hot day, wander down to the lakeshore, sink into the cool clean waters of Lake Geneva, and gaze at the Alps, towering in the distance.

The Lavaux region is made up of nearly 2,051 acres (830 ha) of terraced vineyards that stretch along its coastal hills.

THE RHEINSTEIG TRAIL

Castles, Palaces, and Wine on the Rhine

DISTANCE: 200 miles (320 km) point to point   **LENGTH OF TRIP:** 2 to 3 weeks
BEST TIME TO GO: Spring through fall   **DIFFICULTY:** Moderate

There's fierce competition for the distinction of the most beautiful hiking trail in Germany, but the Rheinsteig holds its own among many. Between Bonn and Wiesbaden, it runs nearly 200 miles (320 km) from the gentle, verdant Siebengebirge Mountains, along the Rhine River, the UNESCO World Heritage site Upper Middle Rhine Valley, and finally through the wine-growing region of Rheingau. While it's possible to hike for hours without seeing another person, the walk is most notable for its combination of pleasant river scenery and cultural heritage. One of the most historic regions in Germany, the Rhine area boasts some 60 castles and palaces, many of which hikers may visit or even stay in overnight.

Fall is the most popular time to hike the Rheinsteig, as the countryside and vineyards are transformed into an array of autumn colors, but the paths are generally open year-round. Other seasons also offer their distinctive charms, like the blooming fruit trees of spring. Because camping isn't allowed along the trail—except in official campgrounds—most hikers hit the hay in hotels in trim historic villages and towns along the way. With impeccable signage, it's almost impossible to get lost, and plenty of services cater to hikers. Some businesses will transfer your luggage from hotel to hotel, and there are even benches and shelters built at scenic junctures for civilized breaks or picnics.

CULTURAL HIGHLIGHT

The wine region of Rheingau sits on a south-facing slope of the Rhine as it bends from Lorch to Wiesbaden. Warm summers and gentle winters conspire to make this region perfect for growing Rieslings, which produce a sweet, fruity white often light in alcohol content and rich in *terroir*.

OPPOSITE: Ehrenfels Castle, built in 1212, sits above the Rhine Gorge between Rüdesheim and Assmannshausen.

NEXT PAGES: Katz Castle was built in 1371 and restored in the mid-19th century.

Contrary to what one might think, however, this river valley trail is far from flat. Because the trail meanders up and down the undulating slopes, it's known as a training ground for trekkers preparing to go to the Alps. As you walk along the eastern shore through thick forests of oak and beech, and steep, orderly vineyards, stop to check out wonders like Pfalzgrafenstein, an imposing castle built on a small island in the middle of the Rhine that dates to the 14th century, or the stone-wall ruins of 12th-century Löwenburg castle, which stands atop a 1,493-foot (455-m) mountain with magnificent views. You might also take a detour to the Marksburg castle. Mostly built between the 13th and 15th centuries, it is the only hilltop castle along the Rhine that has never been destroyed (and rebuilt).

Beyond the imposing architecture of this storied valley, the trail has all sorts of smaller

ALTERNATIVE ROUTE

On the opposite, western, side of the Rhine, another hiking trail, the RheinBurgenWeg, follows along the river's shores. At about 120 miles (200 km), it's shorter than the Rheinsteig and traverses much of the same scenery, including vineyards and castles. To sample each trail, hop back and forth between shores on ferries.

ABOVE: In Bacharach, grab a bite to eat at the charming medieval timber-framed Altes Haus, located in the city center.

OPPOSITE: Pass by vine-yards and ripening grape-vines in Rheingau, one of Germany's 13 designated wine regions.

delights in store. Take your time and stop to buy fruit from a local farmer or idly listen to birdsong or inspect a wildflower. Stroll through the streets of villages lined with perfectly kept homes and immaculate storefronts, then laze on the banks of a stream deep in the forest, taking in the scents of wood and loam, and the sounds of moving water. And don't miss famous sights like the Lorelei, a huge rock formation that has been the muse for writers and composers for centuries—and the site where a mythical gorgeous maiden despaired over a cheating lover, threw herself into the river, and turned into a spirit, luring fishermen to their doom. Like a fairy-tale land, the Rhine is full of legends of spirits and nymphs. But, luckily, the conveniences of the modern era are always close at hand: No matter how far you walk, it's generally fairly easy to hop a train or boat all the way back to where you began.

ELBE SANDSTONE MOUNTAINS

The Artists' Inspiration

DISTANCE: 70 miles (112 km) point to point   **LENGTH OF TRIP: 8 days**
BEST TIME TO GO: Spring and fall   **DIFFICULTY: Moderate**

From the late 18th to the mid-19th centuries, Romantic artists often sought their muses in nature. For German painters, musicians, and writers, one easily accessible source of inspiration was the Elbe Sandstone Mountains, a repository of fantastical rock formations and forests just a few miles from Dresden, a center for the art elite.

Today, a 70-mile (112-km) circuit leads around these otherworldly mesas, gorges, spires, and other rock formations in eight well-organized stages. Hikers typically stay in villages where local businesses offer overnight lodging, luggage shuttles, and packed lunches, making the entire trip easy, seamless, and civilized. Interpretive signs along the way even display some of the historic works of art inspired by the landscape.

The trail is a pleasant and ever entertaining mishmash of cultural sights and delightful vistas of nature as it wends through a mix of forests, gorges, mountains, and villages. The first stage, for instance, leads from Pirna-Liebethal, past a memorial to Richard Wagner, near a 1789 castle known for its concerts, through a dark canyon and cave, and finally to the picture-perfect town of Wehlen, situated on the banks of the Elbe.

Some hikers choose to tick off only one or just a few of the trail's eight stages but the entire route offers a parade of surprises. On the second day, for example, it leads up into the hills to viewpoints over soaring finger-like

OPPOSITE: Breathtaking stops, like the Lichtenhain waterfall, await along the 70-mile (112-km) circuit.

NEXT PAGES: Find spectacular views of the Elbe River winding through the Elbe Sandstone Mountains from the scenic overlook Basteiaussicht at Bastei.

WHAT YOU'LL SEE: Rock formations | Caves |
Stone bridges | Historic guesthouses
and mills | Königstein Fortress

pinnacles and cliffs, skirted in their finest green-ery. Tiptoe across stone bridges and wooden steps, and travel through narrow ravines and past a grotto carpeted in lush ferns and moss. Stop in an 1830s guesthouse and hop a ride on a tram that has been operating since 1898.

From time to time, views over the countryside and jagged rock formations arise only for hikers to plunge back into the valleys dotted with historic mills, immaculate Saxon Swiss houses, bakeries, and restaurants that are happy to cater to walkers—even sweat-encrusted ones. Plenty of bratwurst, sauerkraut, and beer are on offer as well as regional dishes like *krautwickel* (stuffed cabbage with minced meat) and *kartoffelsuppe* (potato soup).

One notable stop is the Königstein Fortress, a compound that has dominated the countryside for more than 400 years. But perhaps what astounds most is the natural landscape itself. It may have been inhabited for centuries, but the views over the alien-like formations feel surprisingly untamed.

POST-HIKE ACTIVITY

One nice perk of traveling the Malerweg is the spa towns, such as Gohrisch, Rathen, and Bad Schandau, along the way. The latter sits conveniently at the end of the fifth stage of the route. After dinner, sink into the beautifully lit pools at Bad Schandau's Toskana Therme and wash away the day's aches.

MOUNT SKÅLA

Norway's Natural Staircase

DISTANCE: **10 miles (16 km) out and back**   **LENGTH OF TRIP:** **4 to 6 hours**
BEST TIME TO GO: **Summer**   **DIFFICULTY:** **Strenuous**

If you've hiked towering peaks and plunged into canyons, and are in search of your next challenge, consider Norway's 6,063-foot (1,848-m) Mount Skåla. This peak boasts the country's longest continuous uphill trail, which wends from the foot of a fjord up some 6,000 thigh-incinerating vertical feet (1,800 m) to a high exposed peak with mind-bending views of the fjords, mountains, and glaciers that coastal Norway is famous for.

The trail ascends so quickly that the climate can change dramatically, going from T-shirt weather at the bottom to frigid jacket temperatures up top. It's not uncommon for snowfields to dot the upper slopes of the hike, even in summertime, which means it's critical to bring good boots and warm layers—you might even be glissading down the snowfield on the way back down.

Hikers start in mellow green pastures sprinkled with cows and pass a series of waterfalls as they climb up through leafy forests, keeping an eye out for the admiral butterfly, red deer, and birds like the gray-headed woodpecker. Eventually, trekkers ascend past tree line, where views extend over the sea and steep slopes of these ancient fjords. The gravel and stone-step path is exceptionally well maintained. As you climb up rocks and steps, notice the hardy alpine plants, like crowberries and heather, and, finally, barren rocky slopes inhabited only by lichen and moss. The last stretch is often covered in a long snowfield before you reach a ridgeline of talus.

OPPOSITE: Built in 1891, the rustic cabin at Mount Skåla's peak was once a retreat for tuberculosis patients; it can now sleep up to 22 hikers.

NEXT PAGES: A marked path winds up the mountain, leading to panoramic views and the overlook cabin.

Fjords I Glaciers I Cows I Waterfalls I Admiral butterflies I Red deer I Gray-headed woodpeckers I Cowberries I Heather I Lichens I Mosses

You know you've made it when you come to Kloumann Tower, a round stone hut built in 1891 by a doctor who wanted to encourage Norwegians to get out into the fresh air. Hikers have stayed in the old damp stone tower for decades—and still do in the summer—but in 2016, the Norwegian Trekking Association built an attractive new cabin that looks straight out of a design magazine, with blond-wood interiors, enormous picture windows with views of the mountains, and bunks with big fluffy duvets. Out of kind consideration for their quadriceps muscles, many hikers rest here for the night, cooking their own food, chatting with other hikers, perhaps playing games or taking a moment to toast each other and the natural beauty. From the hut, watch as the long light of the north slowly drains from the sky, alpenglow paints the peaks a warm shade of peach, and the horizon surrenders from pink and purple to the deep blue of night.

ALTERNATIVE ROUTE

While most visitors come to Skåla between June and September, a hardy bunch of *randonée*—also known as alpine-touring—skiers arrive in the winter months. They follow the same steep trail on skis and stay in the same cabin, but arc sweeping turns across the mountain on the way down.

REINEBRINGEN, LOFOTEN ISLANDS

Small Mountain, Big View

DISTANCE: Less than 1.5 miles (2.5 km) out and back   **LENGTH OF TRIP:** 1.5 to 2 hours
BEST TIME TO GO: Summer   **DIFFICULTY:** Moderate

Reinebringen may be little, but she is fierce. Overlooking the fishing hamlet of Reine in Norway's Lofoten Islands, this peak stands only 1,470 feet (448 m) high, but is renowned as the best view on the islands. It has also been known for the exceedingly dangerous trail that beelines up its vertiginous south-facing slope. So many visitors were falling on the loose, steep, slippery trail that locals set up a warning sign at the bottom encouraging them not to venture up. Luckily, in 2016, the local municipality and an outdoor organization stepped in and hired a crew of Nepalese Sherpas to build a trail of stairs to the top, which is slated to be completed in 2020.

On the new trail, visitors will climb this legendary peak in relative safety—although that's not to say that your muscles won't endure discomfort on the 1,500 stone steps that lead to the summit. From a meandering path through birch forests, the trail quickly ascends above tree line. Where the slope steepens, an outrageous view unfolds. Jagged ridges and steep mountainsides plummet into the shiny deep-blue sea that, from above, appears silky and perfectly smooth. The immaculate houses of Reine freckle the harbor far below and boats ply the water, leaving wakes like delicate white threads. A fjord stretches into the distance and steep, mountainous islands dot the sea beyond.

WHAT YOU'LL SEE: Birch forest | Fjords | Sea and island views

ALTERNATIVE ROUTE

The Lofoten Islands are packed with great hikes. On the island of Vestvågøy, try the 3.7-mile (6-km) trail up Justadtinden, a 2,421-foot (738-m) peak. The route leads through gentle grassy hills then up steeper, rockier slopes to a wide summit with 360-degree views over peaks, lakes, and the dark-blue sea.

From the edge of Reinebringen hikers can take in dazzling views of Kirkefjord, the village of Reine, and Reinevatnet lake.

SAREK NATIONAL PARK

A Great Wilderness in Northern Europe

DISTANCE: 40-plus miles (60-plus km) point to point   **LENGTH OF TRIP:** 7-plus days
BEST TIME TO GO: Late summer and early fall   **DIFFICULTY:** Expert-only

Europe is not known for its huge open spaces and megafauna, which is why Sarek National Park, which protects 761 square miles (1,971 sq km) in Sweden's far north is such a wondrous surprise. The semi-nomadic Sami people have lived in the region known as Lapland, practicing reindeer husbandry, gathering berries, and maintaining rich cultural traditions, since time immemorial, but their impact on the land has been minimal. The result is a pristine collection of 6,000-foot (2,000-m) peaks (including six of Sweden's highest mountains), sprawling valleys, beautiful forests, brawny rivers, lakes, and nearly 100 glaciers—a wilderness that appears untouched by human hands.

Traveling here is not for wilderness beginners. There are few trails over this rugged terrain, and the weather can oscillate from desperately hot to cold and stormy, even in the middle of summer. At times, hikers face battalions of mosquitoes and traverse icy rivers and slippery snowfields as they make their way across vast expanses of treeless tundra.

But for those with map-and-compass skills—or a good guide—many rewards await. Chart your own custom overland route in one of Europe's last wildernesses and savor people-free solitude for days. You'll see great herds of reindeer crossing the land, moose wading and munching in the shallows of swamps, and, if you're very lucky, even a wolverine high in the mountains.

OPPOSITE: A herd of semi-domesticated reindeer tramp through the snow.

NEXT PAGES: Established in 1909, Sarek National Park protects a delta landscape, vast mountain peaks, nearly 100 glaciers, and the homeland of the Sami people.

"This is pure nature," says William Gilman, the founder of True Nature Sweden, a guide service that offers trips to Sarek and neighboring Padjelanta National Park. "There isn't a single ready-made thing for tourists. You can't use your phone. It's just being in pure wilderness."

Over the days, your nervous system relaxes as you sync with the rhythms of the land and the sun. Watch as the slanting northern light constantly changes over the day, painting the landscape different colors. In summer, the sunlight persists well into the small hours of night. Underfoot, marvel at the small, fierce plants that survive in this harsh climate. You likely won't see Sami people with their reindeer herds, but hidden evidence of human occupation dates to at least 7,000 years ago. In the middle of this unbroken swath of tundra, it's poignant to reflect on a community that left the land so gorgeously intact.

WILDLIFE SPOTTING

Reindeer, called caribou in North America, make northern ecosystems tick, providing food for all sorts of creatures, including humans. There are two varieties—tundra and woodland. Tundra reindeer migrate as far as 3,000 miles (4,828 km). To combat the great northern cold, reindeer have hollow hairs for insulation and deeply cloven hoofs so they don't sink too deep into the snow.

GLENINCHAQUIN PARK

A Hidden Emerald Valley in County Kerry

DISTANCE: 2.5 miles (4 km) in a loop **LENGTH OF TRIP:** 1.5 to 2 hours
BEST TIME TO GO: Summer **DIFFICULTY:** Easy

Gleninchaquin Park, a farm and reserve on the northwest shore of Ireland's Beara Peninsula, is only 1,500 acres (600 ha) but offers a quiet, peaceful immersion into the Irish landscape of yore. This glaciated valley features bright-green meadows, some dotted with sheep and goats, a spectacular 460-foot (140-m) cascading waterfall, streams with log bridges, and stone paths that lead up into wild areas with views over pewter lakes. If it weren't for the narrow five-mile (8-km) tar-and-chip road to get to the park's entrance, which precludes large buses, this place would likely be mobbed.

Thankfully, visitors often have the six serene trails to themselves, which range from short, flat strolls to heart-pumping rambles. Try the Red Walk, also called "Over the Waterfall," which leads 2.5 miles (4 km) up the mountain to two glacial lakes with views over the lush patchwork countryside and Kenmare Bay. Watch the shadows of clouds pass over the landscape below. Then descend to the top of the waterfall and along the river with its series of rock-ensconced pools. After the rugged mountain trail, the stroll by the river, with the sounds of birdsong and trickling water, can feel as peaceful as a natural Zen temple.

WHAT YOU'LL SEE: Waterfalls | Meadows | Sheep | Glacial lakes | Kenmare Bay

ALTERNATIVE ROUTE

The mellow Heritage Trail leads to an 18th-century stone-and-thatch cottage that was abandoned in 1898 but recently restored. Here, in the 19th century, families eked a living off the land through farming. Now, the farmstead is so picturesque that it has made cameos in fashion magazines, as well as the film *The Widow's Last* about the Irish famine.

Handcrafted bridges can be found along the River Walk, which leads to a series of rock pools and picturesque waterfalls.

THE DINGLE WAY

An Immersion in Ancient and Contemporary Irish Life

DISTANCE: 111 miles (179 km) in a loop   **LENGTH OF TRIP: 6 to 9 days**
BEST TIME TO GO: Late spring through early fall   **DIFFICULTY: Moderate**

Human beings have dwelled in the rolling hills and along the rowdy coasts of Ireland's Dingle Peninsula for some 6,000 years, leaving behind a plentiful trove of ancient homes, forts, and artifacts. It may be the richest collection of visible archaeological remains in the country, and the Dingle Way, which circles this rural thumb of land, is a prime way to see them.

Along this route, which includes both roads and trails, hikers explore promontory forts, where Bronze Age communities staved off invaders, and even more ancient earthen ring forts that once protected small collections of mud-and-wattle houses, now long gone. Scattered across the countryside in some areas are early Celtic crosses, Celtic churches, conical dome-shaped stone structures known as beehive huts, and ogham stones, obelisks etched with an early form of written language.

Rich with history, this land is also full of vitality and variety—and outstanding mountain and ocean views. Along footpaths and empty country roads known as *boreens*, hikers pass through some of the world's oldest mountains, including a steep huff up the flank of Mount Brandon, along wild beaches, wide-open moors, and farmland sprinkled with sheep and stone cottages. It's not uncommon for hikers to meet herds of cows and encounter farmers who might give them advice. Some even still speak Irish as their native

POST-HIKE ACTIVITY

For those who wish to take their time, the town of Dingle makes an excellent stop for a day's layover. Situated on the sea, it's lined with tidy and colorful little homes and often comes alive with traditional Irish music in the evenings—and, naturally, the age-old pub life that Ireland is known for.

OPPOSITE: The stone Gallarus Oratory is one of the most famous landmarks on the Dingle Peninsula.

NEXT PAGES: Small villages, where hikers can often find homestays, dot the wild coastline along the Dingle Way.

WHAT YOU'LL SEE: Bronze Age forts and
houses | Celtic crosses and churches |
Wild beaches | Moors | Farmland

tongue—but are conversant in English, too. Many other locals are also happy to offer directions and recommendations, especially on whether to proceed if there's inclement weather, as well as stories about their area's unique history.

Some hikers camp in designated sites while others pitch tents in empty areas. (It's best to ask a farmer's permission, however. Often, they say yes.) But since it rains frequently here and the skies see constantly shifting fog, winds, and occasional sunshine, most opt to stay in the inns, bed-and-breakfasts, and farm guesthouses that dot the small villages along the way. Staying in a village also offers the opportunity to spend the evening in the pub drinking Guinness and swapping stories, two hallowed Irish pastimes. During the day, you might also peruse shops for local artwork.

The Dingle Way is known for its window into rural and ancient life, but it also surprises walkers

KNOW BEFORE YOU GO

Rain is common here, so invest in a good set of waterproof clothing. It's also wise to bring ankle-high hiking boots to keep your feet dry while crossing bogs, a common ecosystem along the Dingle Way. Because the bogs are oxygen poor, they preserve artifacts. Ancient swords, centuries-old stores of butter, and other treasures have been found in these areas.

ABOVE: **With farms along the way, hikers often encounter domesticated animals, like donkeys.**

OPPOSITE: **Local beer, fine whiskey, a leather shop, and live music have been on tap at Dick Mack's Pub since 1899.**

with its wildness. Linda Woods, a hiking guide who founded the outfitter Ireland Walk Hike Bike in 1994, often persuades her clients to take time to stop, sit down, and simply listen, just to hear the silence. "It's this wonderful sense of nothing," she says. "You just hear nothing but nature."

What seem like hundreds of shades of green enliven the pastures and mountains. The path often edges onto beaches or high seaside cliffs, offering views of the many moods of the sea, which influences all aspects of life on this peninsula, from the weather to the cuisine. And on the western end of the peninsula, you can see out to the ocean beyond.

"The western tip is just glorious," says Woods. "You have the sense that you're falling off into the Atlantic Ocean. You have this magnificent view of ocean and waves and the Blasket Islands, then nothing but wide-open ocean and the next stop is America."

ICELAND

KRISTÍNARTINDAR MOUNTAIN

In the Land of Giants

DISTANCE: 11 miles (17.9 km) round-trip   **LENGTH OF TRIP: 6 to 8 hours**
BEST TIME TO GO: Summer   **DIFFICULTY: Strenuous**

Southern Iceland, with its vast black-sand beaches, jewel-tone glacial lagoons, waterfalls, and rowdy seas is a land of extremes. Numerous trails and overland routes lead through the wild expanses of tundra, but one standout is the hike to the top of Kristínartindar, a mountain in the Skaftafell wilderness area of Vatnajökull National Park. With more than 3,000 vertical feet (more than 1,000 m) of elevation gain and a steep, slabby, loose, hair-raising summit climb, it's also a tantalizing challenge.

Traveling in a clockwise direction on the loop trail, hikers are quickly rewarded for their efforts when they reach Svartifoss, a striking waterfall surrounded by unusual dark, columnar basaltic rock formations. From there, head up to a grassy treeless plateau where enormous views unfurl over ridgelines and a glacial valley. The vast topography can easily make one feel blissfully Lilliputian. Continue on, contouring around the plateau to reach a saddle, from which the trail turns loose and steep in parts, requiring clambering with both feet and hands—and a fair bit of nerve. But the top of Kristínartindar affords a view over a tableau of glacial wonders, from steepsided mountains to silty braided rivers, the multicolored tongues of the Skaftafell and Morsár glaciers, and the cold, black ocean in the distance.

WHAT YOU'LL SEE: Waterfalls I Basaltic rock formations I Glaciers

ALTERNATIVE ROUTE

The booming waterfall of Skogafoss is an unmissable attraction on Iceland's south coast. But many visitors don't realize that the trail that heads up its right side leads to more wonders hidden in the valley behind. The trail runs about 16 miles (26 km) to two huts through a cleft roaring and tinkling with cascades.

From the ragged peaks of Kristínartindar, look out over the vast and wild Vatnajökull National Park landscape.

TRYFAN MOUNTAIN

A Legendary Scramble in Snowdonia

DISTANCE: About 2 miles (3.2 km) round-trip   **LENGTH OF TRIP:** 3 to 6 hours
BEST TIME TO GO: Late spring through early fall   **DIFFICULTY:** Strenuous

From below, the charismatic profile of 3,008-foot (917-m) Tryfan, named for its three-finned summit block, appears dark and forbidding. But to some, this vertiginous beast sings a siren call. Tenzing Norgay and Edmund Hillary, the first people to reach the summit of Mount Everest, in 1953, used the peak as a training ground. Today, rock climbers and aspiring mountaineers flock here to test their courage on its exposed slopes.

"It's a great challenge for people who have done some hill walking but want to spread their wings and do some scrambling," says Richard Bale, a Bethesda, Wales–based mountain instructor and founder of Snowdonia Walking and Climbing. "It's a really good, solid route and it's also very accessible."

The most popular way to the peak, up the north ridge, quickly turns vertical like a natural jungle gym. With hands at the ready, climb up through gullies and along ribs of rock, past a famous horizontal cannon-like formation—a favorite photo op. At the top, two large boulders named Adam and Eve sit about three or four feet (1–1.2 m) apart. The bravest (or perhaps most foolhardy) climbers leap between them. Or simply take in the vistas of the Ogwen Valley, the mountains, and Liverpool Bay as they appear between the clouds.

WHAT YOU'LL SEE: Ogwen Valley | Liverpool Bay | Goats | "Adam and Eve" boulders

POST-HIKE ACTIVITY

Originally built in 1810 as a mountain farmhouse, the Pen-Y-Gwryd Hotel hosted climbers from the 1953 Everest expedition while they trained in Snowdonia. Today, mountaineers and hikers still stay in the hotel, gather around the lobby's fireplace, and swap tales of adventure in the bar. The hotel also maintains a collection of historic climbing memorabilia.

As the sun sets, Tryfan—the 15th tallest mountain in Wales—casts its shadow over the Ogwen Valley.

SOUTH WEST COAST PATH

An Epic Journey Along England's Southwest Coast

DISTANCE: 630 miles (1,014 km) one way   **LENGTH OF TRIP:** 6 to 8 weeks
BEST TIME TO GO: Spring through fall   **DIFFICULTY:** Strenuous

Starting in the early 1800s, England's coastguards patrolled the country's shoreline on foot, looking for smugglers in every harbor and cove. Now, in the counties of Somerset, Devon, Cornwall, and Dorset, their routes form the South West Coast Path, the country's longest national hiking trail.

The path doesn't take the most direct route, and that's a good thing. It wends along seaside cliffs, down through historic fishing villages, and up through moorlands and heaths as it circumnavigates England's blustery and dramatic southwestern peninsula. Today, the trail's acolytes include everyone from hardy marathon runners tackling the entire trail in 10 days to Sunday strollers who amble between tea shops and pubs, drinking in cider, beer, cream tea, and plenty of coastal scenery.

Whatever your speed or ambition, the trail has a wide diversity of attractions. The Jurassic Coast, a 95-mile (153-km) stretch of shore in Devon and Dorset, showcases rock formations shaped over hundreds of millions of years, including imposing sea stacks, a sea arch, and a 17-mile-long (27.5-km) natural barrier beach, one of the longest of its kind in Europe. (It's not uncommon for beachcombers to find fossils here.) Thanks to the area's rich human history, hikers can also spot the subtle earthworks of ancient hill forts, rough stone Roman-era chapels, and medieval churches. Fortifications from ancient times

WILDLIFE SPOTTING

While the path isn't known for its showy wildlife, numerous species can be spotted with a keen eye. Peregrine falcons nest on many of the cliffs. Watch as they dive in incredible "stoops" while hunting for prey. From shore, hikers occasionally spot seals, dolphins, and even basking sharks in the navy blue waters below.

OPPOSITE: Spring primroses and violets bloom along the Hangman Hills.

NEXT PAGES: Wander along chalk cliffs and gaze at the sea stacks at Old Harry Rocks on the Jurassic Coast.

WHAT YOU'LL SEE: **Cliffs I Sea arches and stacks I Beaches I Fossils I Roman-era chapels I Medieval churches I Historic forts**

to the Victorian era and even World War II dot the coast. In some places, the coastguard cottages and walls still remain.

Even though the trail is never all that far from civilization and hugs the shoreline, it undulates mercilessly, ascending (and descending) nearly four times the height of Everest over its 630 miles (1,014 km). It crosses numerous streams, rivers, and estuaries, some of which can be traversed on footbridges. Others require a short ferry ride. And while parts of the path run through busy tourist towns bustling with hotels, stores, restaurants, and ice cream shops, other areas are surprisingly wild, such as the north Devon coast. For walker Raynor Winn, author of the best-selling memoir *The Salt Path*, which tells the story of how she and her husband coped with tragedy by hiking the trail, it was this proximity to nature that was most healing.

"The path, the cliffs, the sea, the endless horizon—that's what attracted us," she says. "It was

KNOW BEFORE YOU GO

While the South West Coast Path can be walked any time of year, the most popular times are spring and early summer, when flowers emerge, lambs dot the meadows, and vivid shades of green brighten the landscape. In summer, the trail becomes busy. Fall is quieter; the water is warmer and autumn colors emerge.

ABOVE: In Devon, Docton Mill Gardens and Tea Room offers award-winning cream teas and homemade treats.

OPPOSITE: Boats dock at Polperro, a fishing village and civil parish of the Polperro Heritage Coastline in south Cornwall.

the most incredible sense of freedom." Winn found the trail remarkably unpredictable, with jaw-dropping surprises, from the ferocity of the sea and the weather at Land's End, the westernmost point in England, to the magical experience of taking a dip in a secluded cove and swimming with a pod of passing dolphins. One day, clouds of ladybugs hatched, alighted on her and her husband's hands and took off from their fingertips. On another day, they watched a landslide wash reddish cliffs into the sea, turning the waves into a boiling cauldron of crimson. Most of all, hikers relish the freedom of being immersed in nature in a land so long inhabited by human beings.

"We were just so absorbed by the incredible landscape, it became almost like a walking meditation," Winn says. "Each step became a reason to take the next and the next."

THE VIA DINARICA

A High Tour of the Western Balkans

DISTANCE: 783 miles (1,260 km) one way   **LENGTH OF TRIP:** 7 to 12 weeks
BEST TIME TO GO: Late spring, summer, and early fall   **DIFFICULTY:** Strenuous

The Western Balkans are defined by their rugged, mountainous landscapes and a long history of wars, conquests, shifting religions, and visiting peoples. Still opening to tourism, the region's spectacular wildernesses and pastoral villages are remarkably well preserved, and the Via Dinarica, a long-distance trail traversing eight countries, is like an all-access pass to the best of them.

Technically, the Via Dinarica isn't one trail but three long-distance paths that link ancient routes with newly built connectors. The blue trail follows the coastline, the green trail threads through forests and valleys, and the white trail winds through the high zones, ascending some of the tallest peaks in each country. So far, the white trail is the only one that has been completed, running some 783 miles (1,260 km) and ascending and descending more than 160,000 feet (50,000 m).

On its trip through the Balkans, the white trail of Via Dinarica crosses numerous white limestone mountains and karsts of various shapes and heights, deep beech forests, high meadows packed with wildflowers, glacial lakes, and remote communities where locals still live and work on farms and in pastures. In some areas, hikers camp. In others, they stay in lodgings from remote huts to family guesthouses. Between communities, it's possible to see deer, bear, and chamois, a native antelope. Also keep

ALTERNATIVE ROUTE

For those who prefer their mountains with a healthy dose of sea, consider hiking the blue route of the Via Dinarica on Croatia's Adriatic Coast. This section passes through white karsts with views of the coast, traverses attractive villages, and even crosses four Croatian islands accessible via bridges.

OPPOSITE: The Veliki Prštavac Waterfall is the second highest cascade in Plitvice Lakes National Park.

NEXT PAGES: Famous for its wool, Lukomir, the oldest village in Bosnia, sits 4,921 feet (1,500 m) above sea level on Bjelašnica mountain.

an eye out for foxes, rabbits, snakes, or even a wild boar. Hikers say that the undiscovered nature of this path and the encounters with enthusiastic locals are some of the highlights of the trek.

In some places, "You can hike for days without seeing anyone," says Sabina Sirco, a guide who leads trips on the Via Dinarica for Green Visions, a Sarajevo-based travel company, and writes about the trail at wildinthebalkans.com. "Local people are inviting you to camp in their garden. Often they don't know English, but they're cooking something delicious for you." Some days, you'll encounter villagers waving from their homes or wordlessly leading you back to the path when you've strayed. Come evening, you might find yourself sitting alongside new friends, washing down home-cured meats with a healthy dose of throat-clearing *rakia,* a fruit brandy popular in the region.

POST-HIKE ACTIVITY

Whitewater streams and rivers ply the gorges of these mountains, and many are accessible to rafters. The Tara River, for example, on the border of Montenegro and Bosnia and Herzegovina, features gemlike turquoise water, winds through the deepest canyon on the continent, and tumbles into a series of Class II–IV rapids.

ABOVE: A boardwalk spans the lower Plitvice lakes and small cascades of the national park, a UNESCO World Heritage site.

OPPOSITE: Autumn fog lingers in a valley below the peaks of the Via Dinarica at sunset.

While the whole trail presents a formidable challenge, the vast majority of hikers choose to tick off smaller sections at a time. In Bosnia and Herzegovina, for example, the hike up Čvrsnica Mountain offers views of dramatic sloping cliffs, deep valleys, and a striking stone arch named Hajdučka Vrata. On the mountain's slopes, an alpine hut named Vilinac sits above tree line and offers lodging and meals to hikers. At sunrise and sunset, the dwindling light paints the landscape of exposed rock and cliffs dramatic hues of peach and gold.

Farther north, Slovenia offers different mountain scenery and historic castles like Predjama, an 800-year-old white fortress that looks straight out of *Game of Thrones*. Legend has it that a brave knight defended the structure for more than a year before succumbing to the betrayal of a servant. The castle, whose armory, chapel, kitchen, and secret tunnel are open to visitors, is a colorful testament to the rich history of this storied region.

WHITE ROCKS AND THE VIHORASKI

A Limestone Fairyland

DISTANCE: 4 miles (6.5 km) one way   **LENGTH OF TRIP:** 6 to 8 hours
BEST TIME TO GO: Summer and early fall   **DIFFICULTY:** Moderate

The region of Gorski Kotar in Croatia is known for its abundance of greens with thick forests and aquamarine rivers spilling into rapids. Nestled deep in the mountains, the White Rocks and Vihorski Trail is a jewel even by international standards. It features an other-worldly landscape of paper-white limestone karsts that jut out of the hilly woodlands like an audience of frozen gnomes. Relatively few tourists travel here—it is reached by about a 2.5-hour drive from Zagreb—but those who do are rewarded with an obstacle-course-like scramble through these striking white thumbs.

"This place has a mystique and a very special feeling," says Petra Ban, lead guide and owner of Natural Croatia Adventure Travel Agency, based in Zagreb. "Everything is so green and just very peaceful and silent."

The trail leads down boulders into little valleys and up on top of monoliths, requiring climbing with hands and feet in some places as well as carefully negotiating ladders. From the White Rocks section to another collection of similar rocks named Samarske, the trail winds through silent forests populated by deer and bears. From time to time, views open up over a densely wooded landscape that appears blissfully unbroken by human hands.

WHAT YOU'LL SEE: Limestone karsts I Deer I Bears I Green valleys I Meadows

POST-HIKE ACTIVITY

Close to the end of the hike, a hut, Rat-kovo Skloniste, is tucked cutely into a half cave. With bunks, a stove, and a cistern of filtered rainwater, this tiny wooden structure makes a prime spot to hit the sack for the evening. Spend the next day climbing around the natural jungle gym of these limestone karsts.

In stunning contrast, eroded limestone peaks—the White Rocks—are surrounded by lush green forest.

ALPE ADRIA TRAIL

From Glaciers to the Sea

DISTANCE: 466 miles (750 km) one way   **LENGTH OF TRIP: 5 to 6 weeks**
BEST TIME TO GO: Late summer   **DIFFICULTY: Moderate**

From the foot of Grossglockner, the highest peak in Austria, to the Italian town of Muggia on the Adriatic coast, the Alpe Adria Trail wends its way ever so gently through European countryside. This trail, established in 2013, is a convenient amalgamation of existing paths that connect the Alps with the sea through three countries: Austria, Slovenia, and Italy. Stewarded by a consortium of nonprofits and businesses, the trail is impeccably well-organized and marked, with interpretive signs along the way and even a central booking service that helps travelers arrange transportation, shuttles, and overnight accommodations. (Camping is not allowed, but each stage ends conveniently at a village or lodge of some kind.)

While only a small number of people aim to complete the entire trail in one go, many tackle day hikes, shorter multiday sections, or complete the trail in stages over a number of years. One 10-day stretch, for example, leads from the very first stage of the trail, at the base of 12,461-foot (3,798-m) Grossglockner, through mountains, meadows, forests, and farmland to Danielsberg in Carinthia, a holy mountain where Celts, Romans, and early Christians have staged ceremonies over the centuries. (Today, a small Romanesque chapel survives.) Along the way, stop in rural villages like Heiligenblut, nestled among peaks with an immaculate church sporting a slim, elegant spire, and at attractions like Falkenstein, a fairy-tale-like castle that sits regally on a

OPPOSITE: A summit cross marks the peak of Gerlitzen mountain in Austria, where climbers take in unforgettable panoramic views.

NEXT PAGES: Italy's Cividale del Friuli sits in the foothills of the eastern Alps near the Slovenian border.

WHAT YOU'LL SEE: Rural villages and farms I
Waterfalls I Tyrolean Dolomites I Vineyards I
Cherry orchards I Oak forests

hilltop. The trail leads past farms, gorges pulsing with waterfalls, and views of the jagged Tyrolean Dolomites. At times, you'll be following in the footsteps of Christian pilgrims.

On the other end of the trail, a six-day trip leads from Cividale del Friuli to the Adriatic seashore in Italy, taking hikers through Italian and Slovenian vineyards, cherry orchards, and oak forests. Diversions abound, from ambling around the red-roofed town of Šmartno, a maze of narrow old-world streets, to lolling about in the nearby rocky pools where local bathers come to cool off. As the trail descends, the cuisine and cultural traditions change from more alpine fare to Mediterranean seafood. Near the coast, take time to stop at a local *osmizze,* a small, homey, countryside tavern, to linger over a glass of wine and savor local meats and *formaggi*. Before departing, stroll the seaside hamlet of Muggia and sunbathe on one of Trieste's comely beaches.

KNOW BEFORE YOU GO

Trekkers on the Alpe Adria Trail stay in lodging overnight rather than camping, which means that their backpacks are delightfully small. What should you bring? A change or two of clothes, toiletries, sunscreen, a bathing suit, flip-flops, a towel for alfresco dips, a first aid kit and—if you like—trekking poles.

PART FOUR

AFRICA

With Mount Kilimanjaro (page 262) as background, a family of springbok antelope graze in the highland grasses.

THE SINAI TRAIL

Walking Alongside the Bedouins

DISTANCE: 340 miles (550 km) one way **LENGTH OF TRIP:** 42 days
BEST TIME TO GO: Spring and fall **DIFFICULTY:** Moderate

The interior of Egypt's Sinai Peninsula is marked by vast desert, shimmering oases, and rich Bedouin cultures, but it has long been avoided by travelers. Many visitors instead go to the area's built-up eastern shore, and most avoid the area altogether because of safety concerns about terrorist activity. But in the mid-2010s, leaders from eight Bedouin tribes, representatives from nongovernmental organizations, and volunteers came together to try to make the area more enticing to tourists by building the Sinai Trail, Egypt's first long-distance path.

The trail, which first opened in 2015 and has since expanded, encircles the peninsula in a triangular shape. The first section that opened leads 155 miles (250 km) from the Gulf of Aqaba to the highlands of St. Catherine, taking most trekkers between 12 and 14 days. (The full circuit stretches 340 miles (550 km) around the peninsula and takes about 50 days to walk.) The first and most popular section of trail passes through wide wadis, low plains, and winding canyons, then ascends into the highlands of the interior. The landscape is undoubtedly harsh and the climate unforgiving, which means that Bedouin guides, with their camels, navigation skills, and intimate knowledge of the land, are critical for a successful hike.

"The Sinai Trail has beautiful expanses of wilderness, but what differentiates it from most trails is that there are people who have lived here for hundreds

POST-HIKE ACTIVITY

The Sinai Peninsula has an enticing menu of outdoor activities. The Red Sea coast is a mecca for divers, and, in the interior, world-class rock climbing is still being developed on sandstone, granite, and limestone crags. The Bedouins also offer courses on medicinal plants of the area.

OPPOSITE: Nasser Monour (right), his son, and Mohammed Abu Ramadan guide hikers through the Saint Catherine Highlands.

NEXT PAGES: With pack camels to lighten their load, hikers make their way along a narrow pass on the Sinai Trail.

of years," says Omar Samra, the first Egyptian to climb Mount Everest and founder of Wild Guanabana, an outfitter that arranges Bedouin-led treks on the Sinai Trail. "The amount of wisdom they have from walking these lands, being in nature so long, and having that pace of life is vast . . . they've got so much to give to us in Egypt—and to the whole world."

On this hike, you'll immerse yourself in the Bedouin homelands. The landscape is marked by heat and aridity, but it's far from bland: Mountains striped with shades of red, brown, and gray rock rise out of the flatlands. From time to time, hikers round a bend and a serene pool of water appears, beckoning for a swim. At the oasis of Ein Hudera, soaring cliffs embrace a beautiful patch of greenery. Hikers also come across rocks inscribed by early Christian pilgrims and Nabataeans some 2,000 years ago and pass through peaceful mountain orchards with pomegranate and almond

KNOW BEFORE YOU GO

It's wise to familiarize yourself with Bedouin customs before you go. For example, both women and men should wear long pants and shirts with sleeves. In holy areas, a head scarf for women is appropriate. Bedouins also have a custom of sharing their food generously—be generous back—and be aware that alcohol is forbidden.

ABOVE: **Traditional Bedouin flower tea is served to tired hikers at a camp in Wadi Tlaah, which is lined with green Bedouin gardens.**

OPPOSITE: **Hikers make their way up a hill in the desert landscape.**

trees that have been tended for more than a millennium. It's rare to see wildlife, but species like falcons, eagles, foxes, and lizards do live here.

One of the highlights is an ascent of Mount Sinai, which has special significance in Judeo-Christian religions as the place where God appeared to Moses and offered him the Ten Commandments. Explore the small Byzantine church at the summit. At the foot of the mountain, the monastery of St. Catherine dates to the mid-500s A.D. Legend holds that it is the oldest working monastery in the world. It is believed that the peninsula has been inhabited since prehistoric times, and that ascetics and mystics were long drawn here.

In the evening, take part in one of the Bedouins' most hallowed traditions: gathering around the campfire for hours, staring at the canopy of stars overhead, and listening as tribal leaders tell a mix of stories both true and mythical, the boundaries between the two blurring in the magic of a desert night.

CAMINO DE LOS GRACIOSEROS

An Airy Route to the Sea

DISTANCE: About 4.7 miles (7.5 km) round-trip   **LENGTH OF TRIP:** 2 to 3 hours
BEST TIME TO GO: Spring and fall   **DIFFICULTY:** Moderate

For more than a century, the residents of La Graciosa—part of the Canary Islands—crossed a strait and traveled a precipitous footpath up the cliffs of Famara to reach the isle of Lanzarote. Today, this path is one of the most striking coastal trails in the Canary Islands, a Spanish archipelago 67 miles (108 km) off the northwest coast of Africa. Not far from the village of Ye in the Las Palmas province of northern Lanzarote, hikers start their journey at about 1,175 feet (358 m) above sea level then descend cobbled and gravelly paths with arresting views over La Graciosa and the turquoise-green strait.

"It is one of the best views of the island," says Gilles Audenaerde, director of One Two Trek, a local guide service. "And the colors are always changing because of the movements of the clouds with the trade winds." Falcons and vultures also soar overhead, and lizards and rabbits scurry about.

On the shore, the route passes by old salt-making lagoons, which have been operating for centuries—possibly since the 16th century—and finally ends at a remote people-free beach, Playa del Risco, which is only reachable by foot or boat. In the subtropical climate, which hovers around 70°F (21°C) year-round, the sparkling blue sea begs for a dip.

WHAT YOU'LL SEE: Salt-making lagoons | Volcanic rocks | Coastal views

POST-HIKE ACTIVITY

Some have called the Canary Islands Europe's answer to Hawaii. Like the American archipelago, Lanzarote has prime adventure activities, including surfing. On the northern coast, where the Gracioseros hike is located, breaks like Famara and La Santa beckon to both locals and foreigners, beginners and advanced wave riders.

La Graciosa island can be seen in the distance when standing atop the Famara Cliffs on Lanzarote.

SIMIEN MOUNTAINS

Ethiopia's Otherworldly Peaks

DISTANCE: About 14 miles (23 km) one way   **LENGTH OF TRIP:** 3 days
BEST TIME TO GO: September through November   **DIFFICULTY:** Moderate

The Walia ibex, gelada monkey, and Simien fox, also known as the Ethiopian wolf, have two things in common: They are incredibly rare, and all are rumored to haunt the mysterious mountains of Simien National Park, a UNESCO World Heritage site. This park, located in northern Ethiopia, protects an unusual collection of geological wonders formed by powerful erosive forces, including jagged peaks, plunging valleys, steep cliffs dropping 5,000 feet (1,524 m) into the airy abyss, and Ethiopia's highest peak, 14,938-foot (4,553-m) Ras Dejen. To add to the wild land and animals, the plant life is positively bizarre, with giant lobelia that can stand some 20 feet (6 m) tall and trees that sport lichen growing as long as four feet (1.2 m) like a Gandalf-esque beard.

"I bring my guests here and some will just stand for a half hour and try to take it all in—it's impossible," says Sam Walker, an archaeologist and guide for Ethio Travel and Tours. "It's just the sheerness of the cliffs and the heights of the mountains and the drops."

Trekking routes trace the edges of the escarpment, lead up to Ras Dejen, and dip into the lowlands. One three-day route, for example, leads from the established camp at Sankeber to similar camps at Geech and finally to Chennek. (It's possible to take a road back to the park entrance or retrace your steps.) Local people have made a living in these high, arid, cold, and

OPPOSITE: Giant lobelias are endemic to Ethiopia. They grow (up to 33 feet/10 m) for 20 years before flowering for the first time.

NEXT PAGES: A gelada monkey perches above the valley on a mountain peak.

WHAT YOU'LL SEE: Bearded vultures |
Walia ibex | Gelada monkeys | Simien foxes |
Raptors | Klipspringers | Golden jackals |
Giant lobelias | Waterfalls

unforgiving conditions for untold time by farming and shepherding. For chilly evenings, bring plenty of warm layers.

Along this route, the trail descends and ascends strenuously along this massive uplift. Waterfalls tumble off the edges of cliffs, and vultures and raptors cruise the skies as views over the falling canyon stretch to the horizon. Chances are good that you'll encounter a troop of gelada monkeys lazily ambling around, their manes wafting in the wind. These baboon-like primates spend their time eating grasses on mountaintops and, as skilled rock climbers, even drop over cliff edges from time to time. Golden jackals, baboons, and klipspringers—a type of small antelope—also haunt this high enclave. Take extra time to soak up the atmosphere in the otherworldly afro-alpine forests, where flowers and freaky-looking plants can make it feel as if you're traipsing through the prehistoric land of dinosaurs.

WILDLIFE SPOTTING

The lammergeier, also known as the bearded vulture, is another impressive species of wildlife found in the Simiens. Its wings stretch some 10 feet (3 m) across and it sports black-and-white stripes on its head and spots on its breast. A scavenger, it sometimes drops bones from great heights to break them open on the rocks.

BIG DADDY DUNE

Climbing the Father of All Dunes

DISTANCE: Between 3 and 4 miles (5–6 km) round-trip   **LENGTH OF TRIP:** 2 to 3 hours
BEST TIME TO GO: Year-round   **DIFFICULTY:** Moderate

For 1,200 miles (1,900 km), the Namib Desert guards the southeastern shore of Africa, covering the entire length of Namibia's coastline. In the Nama language, its name means "an area where there is nothing." Well, not quite *nothing*. Trade routes have crossed this desert to the sea, animals from beetles and snakes to ostriches live in various zones, and a giant field of dunes is one of Namibia's prime tourist attractions. Known as Sossusvlei, these shifting hills of rust-colored sand form an indelible landscape of simple hues: red dunes, blue sky, white flats.

Visitors can climb many dunes but one alluringly challenging one is Big Daddy, which rises to 1,066 feet (325 m). While the climb isn't particularly far, it can be arduous as the sun rises and the sand sinks beneath your feet. From the top, views stretch over the ridges of other dunes as well as Deadvlei, a bleached-white clay pan that harbors the poetic, skeletal remains of camel thorn trees that have been standing dead for centuries. To descend, run, leap, and slide (bring or rent a sand board to really experience a thrill) down the face of the slippery dune all the way to the bottom. While it might have taken you two hours to ascend, the flight down takes an exhilarating and unforgettable 45 seconds.

WHAT YOU'LL SEE: Red-sand dunes | Skeletal remains of camel thorn trees

KNOW BEFORE YOU GO

To reach the top, it's key to start early in the morning to avoid the heat. (And in the stillness of morning, keep an eye out for the tracks of any critters who ventured out onto the vast, undulating surface of the sand in the dark hours.) Also be sure to bring plenty of water, as the dry air saps moisture from the body.

At 1,066 feet (325 m), Big Daddy Dune offers a somewhat challenging summit hike and thrilling descent.

MARGHERITA PEAK

The Mountains of the Moon

DISTANCE: 51 miles (82 km) round-trip   **LENGTH OF TRIP:** 7 to 9 days
BEST TIME TO GO: July through September   **DIFFICULTY:** Expert-only

Equatorial glaciers, 16,000-foot (4,900-m) peaks, and fields bejeweled with giant lobelia are just a few of the wild, unexpected sights visitors find in the Rwenzoris, a little-known mountain range in western Uganda, dubbed the "Mountains of the Moon." This range is compact, high, and often encased in mists, which lend it an eerie mystique. Although the region is still relatively unfrequented by visitors, a growing number are venturing here to see one of Africa's most unusual collections of landscapes—and to attempt the Rwenzoris' technically challenging peaks.

One trekking route leads from the national park trailhead to Margherita Peak, the third highest mountain in Africa, then back in a loop to the trailhead. Starting in the early 2000s, with the help of former poachers who know the forests intimately, locals painstakingly cut routes through the bush and hand-carried supplies to build huts. Still, the route is anything but easy—hikers occasionally sink into waist-high mud and negotiate exposed sections of trail over steep ravines and raging rivers. In other words, it's a true adventure.

"People say it's the toughest thing they've ever done—and the most beautiful," says John Hunwick, an Australian expat and managing director of Rwenzori Trekking, a guide service. "I love going up there in the wet season. It's just stunning with the snow falling on the bright-green plants. In some places you don't get inches of moss, you get *feet* of moss."

HISTORICAL FOOTNOTE

The British explorer Sir Henry Morton Stanley's 1880s expedition was reportedly the first group of European explorers to discover the Rwenzori Range. His 1890 book *In Darkest Africa* is an account of this adventure. In 1906, the Duke of Abruzzi, an Italian mountaineer, scaled the highest summits in the range.

OPPOSITE: Cabins are available for camping within Rwenzori Mountains National Park.

NEXT PAGES: Stunning waterfalls, lakes, and glaciers pepper the park, along with beautiful plant life.

Trekkers start at about 4,760 feet (1,450 m) and gradually ascend, navigating four different ecosystems. Walk through woodlands—inhabited by chimpanzees, black-and-white colobus monkeys, and the Rwenzori turaco, a bird with feathers in vibrant hues of red, blue, and green—then up through bamboo forests. Over the days, you'll hop between tussocks, tiptoe along boardwalks over bogs, slog up steep ridgelines, and scramble up boulder fields. Above the tree line, the landscape resembles something drawn by a child with a preposterous imagination: Across large moorlands, enormous, freaky plants take center stage, including groundsels, heathers, and giant lobelia, which can resemble huge microphones. Waterfalls, swift-moving rivers, and serene high-altitude lakes also dot the trail, known for its steepness.

"I've done a lot of trips and it's in my top five favorites ever," says Mark Gunlogson, president of

WILDLIFE SPOTTING

Because of rampant poaching, chimpanzees were almost wiped out in this area. But, according to locals, they have started to recover. Scan for these close human relatives in the woodlands, where they look for fruit, leaves, and seeds to eat. They are known for being gregarious but also sometimes hostile to each other or competing groups.

ABOVE: **Mount Meru is a popular "warm-up" for trekkers looking to tackle its nearby, taller cousin Kilimanjaro.**

OPPOSITE: **A great blue turaco perches in Nyungwe National Park.**

Mountain Madness, which guides on seven continents and runs trips to the Rwenzoris. "I swear there's maybe five switchbacks in the whole trail—the topography is incredible. And it's one of those rare places where you're going from tropical forest to stepping on glaciers."

Some hikers skip the route up Margherita Peak, which is deep in the range, because it requires considerable mountaineering experience. (The first known ascent was in 1906 by Luigi Amedeo, the Duke of Abruzzi, an Italian prince and famed mountaineer and explorer.) But those who do attempt it travel up glaciers with crampons and axes, walk up an equatorial ice ramp with funky ice formations, and then scramble up the rocky, icy summit cap. From the top, you can see over this bastion of steep alpine peaks and, seemingly incongruously, deep into the lush interior of the Congo Basin.

MASAI MARA

Walking With the Maasai

DISTANCE: 1 to 5 miles (1.5–8 km)   **LENGTH OF TRIP: 1 day**
BEST TIME TO GO: Summer and late winter   **DIFFICULTY: Easy**

When walking through the African bush, it's best to keep at least 100 feet (30 m) between you and any large wildlife. But sometimes, when the wind is at your face and you've been in a quiet reverie, you can happen upon a rhinoceros or an elephant munching away, blissfully unaware of your presence. A word to the wise: Don't make a peep. Unexpected moments like these are what make walking safaris with the Maasai so memorable.

"To me, this is the true safari," says Kent Redding, founder of Africa Adventure Consultants, which offers walking safaris in the Masai Mara based out of camps and lodges. "You don't see as many animals [as you would in a car], but it's way more exciting and way more close to nature. The sights and the sounds and smells are all sharpened and heightened."

The nomadic, pastoral, Maasai people have lived in this part of Kenya—as well as northern Tanzania—since time immemorial, and now their lands are patchworked with community conservancies and liberally salted with safari camps. Many Maasai now work as guides for safari-goers and share their intimate understanding of the land, its cycles, and its life with visitors to the area. As you cross through the high grasses, watch for wild herds of zebra, gazelle, and wildebeest, and scan the ground for signs of the countless stories told through scat and tracks.

WHAT YOU'LL SEE: Rhinoceroses I Elephants I Zebras I Gazelles I Wildebeests I Animal scat and tracks I Maasai homelands

CULTURAL IMMERSION

The Maasai are known for their regal stature, distinctive dress, and rich cultural traditions surrounding livestock herding. For many years, the Maasai subsisted on the meat, milk, and blood of their cattle. Although their practices are now changing, many groups have made a point of safeguarding their most treasured customs.

The Maasai, part of an ancient pastoral culture known for its warriors, often serve as safari guides in their preserved homeland.

MOUNT TOUBKAL, ATLAS MOUNTAINS

Standing Atop Northern Africa

DISTANCE: 27 miles (44 km) round-trip   **LENGTH OF TRIP:** 2 days
BEST TIME TO GO: Spring and fall   **DIFFICULTY:** Strenuous

P lodding up the high slopes of Toubkal, the highest peak in North Africa, under the shroud of predawn darkness, a traveler would be forgiven for being a bit nervous. The air is thin at over 14,000 feet (4,300 m), the night is cold, and the trail is rough and rocky. But from the summit of this 13,665-foot (4,165-m) peak, concerns melt as the first rays of sun illuminate a new day—and the rows of crisp serrated ridgelines of the High Atlas Mountains of Morocco. Toubkal is a favorite among visitors to Morocco—donkey trains and other hikers ply the long, dry, rock-and-gravel paths, and often locals join you on their way up to a shrine mid-mountain.

"Some visitors don't expect high mountains and snow in Africa—and they also don't expect the hospitality of the people," says Mustapha Bouinbaden, guide and owner of Toubkal Trekking Adventures. "The people are always smiling, they joke. In this area, people really welcome tourists."

From refuges high up the mountain, hikers start as early as 3:30 in the morning to make it to the top before sunrise. After taking in the views of the peaks in the soft glow of early morning, start the long trip down to the valley floor as the sun washes the mountain slopes in shades of peach.

WHAT YOU'LL SEE: Donkey trains I Barbary macaques I Barbary sheep I Cuvier's gazelles I Barbary figs I Scilla I Starlings I Lesser kestrels

CULTURAL IMMERSION

Partway up the trail to the top of Toubkal, Sidi Chamharouch is a Muslim shrine with a house-size boulder painted bleach white. It covers—legend has it—the tomb of the king of elves. Pilgrims come here to make offerings and wash with the water to cure sickness or address other misfortunes.

Refuge Toubkal was first constructed in the summer of 1938. It was since rebuilt (in 1999) as a modern space with amenities for climbers.

MOUNT KILIMANJARO

The African Queen

DISTANCE: 43 to 60 miles (70–97 km) round-trip   **LENGTH OF TRIP:** 5 to 8 days
BEST TIME TO GO: Winter and summer   **DIFFICULTY:** Strenuous

Even if Kilimanjaro weren't the tallest peak on the African continent, it would still command a magnetic presence. This 19,340-foot (5,895-m) peak rises as a single impressive massif from the grassy plains of Tanzania and claims the distinction of being the tallest freestanding mountain in the world. Formed by three main extinct volcanoes, one of which still has a permanent ice cap, the mountain is snow-tipped year-round. Kilimanjaro National Park was established in 1973 to protect not only the peak but also diverse ecosystems that cling to its slopes and surroundings, which range from wildlife-packed savannas to moors dotted with bizarre plant species, like giant lobelia and groundsel.

Part of the allure of Kilimanjaro is that it's one of the world's few high peaks that can be ascended without mountaineering equipment or specialized skills, which is why tens of thousands of hikers flock here every year to attempt to reach its summit. Of the half-dozen main routes up the mountain, Marangu is the most popular. Huts house people who set off from the trailhead every day. Other routes, such as Machame and Shira, do not have huts—or the huts are so dilapidated that trekkers must bring camping equipment.

Whichever route you choose, the ascent up the mountain is a mesmerizing journey through different plant zones. At the base, farmers grow coffee, bananas, beans, and other crops in the rich volcanic soil. Next comes lush

KNOW BEFORE YOU GO

The nonprofit Kilimanjaro Porters Assistance Project helps advocate for the ethical treatment of porters, who make their livelihoods by ferrying supplies up the mountain for trekkers. Tour companies are certified and must comply with guidelines that safeguard porters' well-being, such as salary minimums and limits to how much they are asked to carry.

OPPOSITE: At 19,340 feet (5,895 m), Kilimanjaro dominates Tanzania's grassy plains.

NEXT PAGES: Climbers pitch their tents behind senecio trees and lobelia at the Barranco Huts Camp.

WHAT YOU'LL SEE: Kilimanjaro National
Park | Savannas | Moors | Giant lobelias |
Groundsels | Coffee, banana, and bean farms |
Montane forest | Colobus monkeys | Elephants |
Leopards | Buffalo | Antelope

montane forest, where black-and-white colobus monkeys swing in the canopy and elephants, leopards, buffalo, and antelope roam. Still higher, the moorlands take over with Dr. Seuss–like plants popping up out of open fields. Continuing upward, the air thins and the vegetation dwindles as the landscape turns barren and rocky. This mountain desert is mostly marked by mosses and lichens that grip the weather-swept rocks. Finally, hikers reach an Arctic-like landscape of snow and ice that persists year-round and protects the summit of this giant massif. Depending on the route you take, you might see a volcanic plug jutting 300 feet (91 m) into the air or a pit of ash inside a volcanic crater. No matter if you make it all the way to the summit or not—few sights are as memorable as a sunset seen from above the clouds on the roof of Africa.

KNOW BEFORE YOU GO

Because hikers can simply walk up it, Kilimanjaro is chronically underestimated. Altitude sickness is a real danger—go slow, drink plenty of water, and don't shy away from turning around if symptoms like headaches and nausea persist. It's also much colder at the top than many expect. Bring plenty of layers, including insulated coats and a very warm sleeping bag.

MOUNT MERU

Kilimanjaro's Not-So-Little Sister

DISTANCE: 30 miles (48 km) round-trip **LENGTH OF TRIP:** 3 days
BEST TIME TO GO: Summer and winter **DIFFICULTY:** Strenuous

Kilimanjaro is the tallest peak in Africa, but it is often ensconced in clouds and invisible to those standing in its shadow far below. That's why there may be no better place to view Africa's great queen than from the top of Mount Meru, a volcanic cone that rises out of the plains some 42 miles (68 km) southwest. From this vantage point, at nearly 15,000 feet (4,600 m), one can often see Kilimanjaro's iconic profile elegantly draped in layers of clouds.

While Meru is a smaller peak, she is no less magnificent and distinctive. On one side, an ancient volcanic eruption blasted a gaping hole, creating a distinctive U-shaped crater and summit ridge. "It looks like what I imagine the moon or Mars to look like—it's really raw and jagged," says Kent Redding, founder of Africa Adventure Consultants, which guides the climb. "This mountain is freestanding and almost perfectly conical—it's just an incredibly impressive peak." While Meru is shorter, less expensive, and less crowded than Kilimanjaro, it's not a cakewalk. It requires ascending more than 10,000 feet (3,048 m), walking at high altitudes, and negotiating narrow trails with steep drop-offs.

Starting in the valley below, hikers will first drive through coffee and banana plantations that grow in the fertile volcanic soil. In the national park, giraffes, Cape buffalo, elephants, warthogs, colobus monkeys, bushbucks, and flocks of birds dwell on the lower slopes of the mountain. As they gain altitude, hikers

OPPOSITE: Zebras graze in the grasslands of Tanzania.

NEXT PAGES: Arusha National Park sprawls out below Mount Meru, near the village of Majengo.

pass through dense montane forests, then through barren rocky mountain desert.

Trekkers typically take three days to climb up Meru, staying in rudimentary huts, Miriakamba and Saddle, which offer bunks along the way. Lovely sights, like waterfalls and the Meru crater, beg for photograph stops. Hikers usually undertake the final push to the top of the peak in the early morning to ensure good weather and plenty of time to make it back down. The finish line is guarded by a hair-raising, tightrope-like walk along a highly exposed summit ridge that's sure to wake anyone out of a half slumber. The prize at the summit is a view over a unique landscape of seemingly endless flat plains and farmland, punctuated by gargantuan volcanic peaks like Kilimanjaro. Sitting on this ragged peak, contemplate the power of these giants as the muted light of early morning paints them in soft hues.

WILDLIFE SPOTTING

Arusha National Park, which protects Mount Meru, has an abundance of wildlife. One of the most dangerous is the Cape buffalo, a relative of the cow. While these massive beasts, weighing up to one ton (900 kg), are grazers and feed primarily on grasses, they can be aggressive. They have been known to trample, gore, and kill even lions.

DOGON COUNTRY

Hiking Into History

DISTANCE: Varies   **LENGTH OF TRIP:** Varies
BEST TIME TO GO: October through January   **DIFFICULTY:** Moderate

To North American eyes, the Bandiagara Escarpment of central Mali resembles the landscape of Utah with its reddish sandstone cliffs, monoliths, and monochrome desert. Here, too, a rich indigenous culture has survived since the Paleolithic era.

The Dogon people are renowned for their animistic religious practices, colorful masks, ceremonial dances, and striking architecture. Nearly 300 communities of mud homes, topped with tapering straw roofs, dot the plateau, cliffs, and plains of Mali's Dogon country. Nestled in cliff alcoves above the Dogon structures, the dwellings, ancient granaries, and burial cocoons of the Tellem people—who lived here centuries ago—also survive. Many travelers have remarked on the intriguing resemblance between Dogon and Tellem structures and the cliff dwellings of the ancestral Puebloan people of the American Southwest.

The best way to immerse oneself in Dogon life is to do as the locals do and walk. A web of footpaths connects the villages, and local guides can lead you along these rugged dirt-and-rock routes. Watch respectfully as women carry big jugs of water on their heads and young kids come out to greet you. Come evening, the mud, clay, and rock dwellings hold onto the day's heat, so follow the locals' lead and clamber onto a roof to fall asleep in the coolness of night under a great salad bowl of stars.

WHAT YOU'LL SEE: Dogon communities | Red sandstone cliffs | Desert | Dogon dwellings | Ancient granaries | Tellem burial sites

CULTURAL IMMERSION

The Dogon know intimately about the movements of the stars. Every 60 years, when the star Sirius rises between two peaks, they hold a special ceremony called Sigi. For three months prior, a group of young men seclude themselves and speak a special language. The next ceremony is expected to happen in 2027.

The Dogon people have built their homes into the cliffside of the Bandiagara Escarpment.

VOLCANOES NATIONAL PARK

Meet the Mountain Gorillas

DISTANCE: 0.5 to 3 miles (0.8–5 km) round-trip   **LENGTH OF TRIP:** 3 to 8 hours
BEST TIME TO GO: Summer and winter   **DIFFICULTY:** Moderate

To approach a mountain gorilla, you must leave everything behind—literally. Once trekkers are close to a group of gorillas in the forest, they stash their packs, water, and food with porters so that they are not mistaken for poachers—and so the animals aren't attracted. Like the famed conservation biologist Dian Fossey, hikers approach with open minds and empty hands (save a camera or two). These sensitive mammals are close genetic relatives to human beings, and many people emerge from an encounter with them touched by their sensitivity, intelligence, and presence.

Only about 1,000 mountain gorillas remain in the wild, and most are clustered in groups around the Virunga Massif, which straddles Rwanda, Uganda, and the Democratic Republic of Congo. Seeing gorillas in their natural habitat requires plunging into the jungle, and the groups in Rwanda's Volcanoes National Park are the most accessible. Rwanda also has exemplary conservation practices and regulates tours to protect the endangered animals. They allow groups of no more than eight hikers and a maximum of 96 visitors per day. (As a result, it's not cheap: A permit to see the gorillas costs $1,500 per day for a foreigner.)

Gorillas roam about looking for fresh bamboo and other vegetation to eat, but trackers can typically find them pretty easily. Depending on where

OPPOSITE: The verdant jungle in Rwanda's Volcanoes National Park makes a protective home for endangered gorillas.

NEXT PAGES: A mountain gorilla nuzzles her baby.

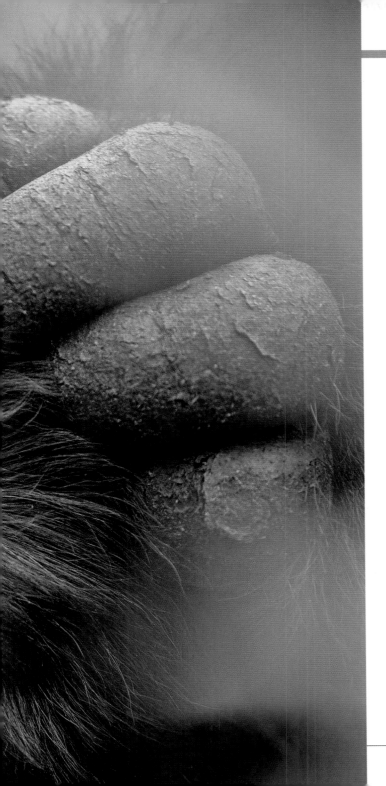

they are—and the weather and mud conditions—visitors might walk for half an hour or much longer, following loose trails through the jungle and often bushwhacking through dense thickets. The slopes can be steep, but the forest has its own beauty, ringing with the sounds of birds.

Groups of gorillas can be as large as a couple dozen individuals, and it's not uncommon to spot babies playing and cavorting. Once trekkers find a group, the Rwandan government allows them to stay and observe for an hour. Keep an eye out for the silverback—the dominant male in the group, weighing up to 450 pounds (200 kg)—and watch as these great apes munch, sleep, loll about, and, occasionally, make eye contact with you.

"Your eyes cross with a gorilla's and something changes inside of you," says Veronica Vecellio, a gorilla senior program manager for the Dian Fossey Gorilla Fund, which helps to protect the animals. "You don't expect this level of connection, this level of understanding of a nonhuman being. It's a life-changing experience."

CULTURAL IMMERSION

The mountain gorillas are a source of national pride. Every year, Rwandan and foreign dignitaries gather for a ceremony in which all the baby gorillas born in the past year are named. And, every morning, musicians and dancers stage a performance to welcome trekkers at the park.

MASOALA NATIONAL PARK

The Biodiversity Hot Spot

DISTANCE: Varies   **LENGTH OF TRIP:** Varies
BEST TIME TO GO: September through December   **DIFFICULTY:** Moderate

Madagascar's landmass drifted apart from other landforms some 60 million years ago, allowing plenty of time for the isolation to give rise to a panoply of marvelously unique creatures and plants. More than 80 percent of the species in the rainforests on the eastern side of the island are endemic. One excellent place to seek out sightings of this legendary wildlife is in Masoala National Park, a peninsula on the northeastern coast where dense rainforests are surrounded by seas teeming with whales, dolphins, turtles, and sharks.

Various routes trace the shores of this peninsula and penetrate the thickly jungled interior, which has been threatened in some places by illegal logging. Hire a local guide to help you navigate the footpaths and spot wildlife. Along the way, you'll likely meet people fishing or tending to livestock, and encounter mud and mind-fraying humidity. With patience and quietude, it's possible to catch sightings of shy and inimitable wildlife. Gape at multicolored geckos, spot a sea turtle taking a breath before disappearing into the sea, or sit in the forest in silence watching a red-ruffed lemur moving slowly and patiently through the trees, eyeing you with heart-melting curiosity.

WHAT YOU'LL SEE: Rainforest I Whales I Dolphins I Sea turtles I Sharks I Geckos I Red-ruffed lemurs I Chameleons

ALTERNATIVE ROUTE

In Antongil Bay, Nosy Mangabe is a small island reserve that protects numerous species, including the aye aye, a rare nocturnal four-pound (1.8-kg) primate with a big bushy tail, large ears, and long fingers. Hike the island's trails by night to find this adorable mammal. By day, see the island's lighthouse and rock inscriptions from 17th-century Dutch sailors.

A male panther chameleon stalks his prey on the beach of Antongil Bay in the national park.

MOUNT MULANJE

A Formidable Massif

DISTANCE: 19 miles (31 km) round-trip   **LENGTH OF TRIP:** 3 days
BEST TIME TO GO: Mid-April through September   **DIFFICULTY:** Strenuous

The giant massif of Mulanje looms over the plains that surround it like an omnipotent presence, inspiring rich spiritual beliefs among locals and providing livelihoods for many thousands of people. While some nearby residents believe that spirits live in the high country and might ferry walkers away, that doesn't stop visitors from venturing up Mulanje's muscly slopes. Legend holds that J.R.R. Tolkien visited Mulanje in the 1930s and was so inspired by the mountain's mystery and magic he used it for the backdrop of his literary worlds. As part of Mount Mulanje's enormous bulk, some 20 peaks soar more than 8,202 feet (2,500 m) high.

Six main trailheads, situated in various villages, and 10 huts (nine are maintained by the Mountain Club of Malawi and the Mulanje Mountain Conservation Trust and Forestry Department) dot the massif. The oldest of the huts—Hope Rest Cottage—dates back to 1899 and is owned by the Church of Central Africa Presbyterian. Numerous alternative trails lead to the granite outcroppings that form the peaks, as well as waterfalls, pools, and plateaus.

The most popular destination for hikers is Sapitwa, the mountain's highest point at 9,849 feet (3,000 m). The loop trip is long enough that most people do it over three days. Although most visitors attempt this between April and September (the rains typically arrive between December and

ALTERNATIVE ROUTE

For those who prefer day hikes, Mulanje has plenty. The walk to the Crater Mouth leads five miles (8 km) round-trip and nearly 1,000 vertical feet (300 m) through old-growth forests and tea fields. Hikers cross two rivers to a depression that is surrounded by vegetation-clad cliffs and peaks.

OPPOSITE: The hike along Mount Mulanje stuns with majestic vistas, jagged peaks, deep gorges, and high grasslands.
NEXT PAGES: The Mulanje Massif disappears into the clouds as a rider cycles a valley road.

WHAT YOU'LL SEE: Cedar trees | Eagles | Buzzards | Ravens | Klipspringers | Streams | Cliffs | Dziwe la Nkhalamba Falls

March), heavy wet mists known as Chiperonis can still roll in between May and August.

Starting in the village of Likhubula, travel the sustained uphill Skyline path through woodlands to a basin where Chambe's imposing east face comes into view. Endemic Mulanje cedar trees live on these slopes and over the course of the hike you might also spot eagles, buzzards, ravens, and the klipspringer, a very small antelope. Mercifully, the incline levels out as it leads to Chambe Hut, which once served foresters on the mountain. Next, on the edge of the Chambe Basin, hikers encounter a knife-edge ridge that divides watersheds and offers vistas of three peaks, Nandalanda, Khuto, and Dzole. Finally, you'll tread over a pass between Chisepo Peak and North Peak to reach Chisepo Hut, the most popular refuge on the mountain, where most peak baggers stage their summit attempts.

EXTRACURRICULAR ACTIVITY

Mulanje's enormous granite faces have few cracks or features, which means they are difficult to climb. The west face of Chambe, however, is an exception with a 5,600-foot (1,700-m) cliff that some say is the longest continuous rock climb in southern Africa. The climb takes at least two days and requires hikers to negotiate rock walls riddled with vegetation—and possibly snakes.

ABOVE: Thuchila Hut, built in 1901, is the oldest shelter on Mount Mulanje. It is an excellent base for mountain scrambling.

OPPOSITE: A waterfall cascades down moss-covered rocks nestled in Mount Mulanje.

In the morning, traveling up the northwest ridge of Sapitwa, hikers trot along big, steep granite slabs that are sticky in nice weather but treacherous in rain. The final stretch leads over an obstacle course of boulders and caves that has, on numerous occasions, been described as "indescribable." From the top, hikers see peaks and ridgelines poking out of a sea of cobblestone-like clouds. On a clear day, it's possible to gaze across the plains, and even to the Indian Ocean coastline of neighboring Mozambique.

On the way back down, travelers stay either in Chambe or Chisepo huts, then spend their last day leisurely walking back down the Chapaluka path, which follows a couple of streams as they tumble down through woods in a narrow valley flanked by impressive cliffs. Dziwe la Nkhalamba Falls, a beautiful waterfall cascading into a boulder-studded pool, is a refreshing (read: cold) spot to wash off the trek's salt and sweat.

ETHIOPIA

ERTA ALE VOLCANO

To the Fiery Gates and Back

DISTANCE: 9 miles (15 km) round-trip   **LENGTH OF TRIP: 2 days**
BEST TIME TO GO: October through June   **DIFFICULTY: Moderate**

The trip to Erta Ale, Ethiopia's largest volcano, can feel a bit risky. Continuously active, it has a living lava lake that has been known to spurt and overflow over the crater rim, sending red-hot ooze flowing downhill in a miraculous stream. Of course, this natural phenomenon is also the prime attraction. To see it with their own eyes, hikers must first travel painstakingly slowly on rough roads over hardened lava, rock, and sand through the Afar region, a punishing desert where temperatures regularly top 110°F (43°C). Then, to avoid the heat of the day, hikers start climbing after dark on rugged, hardened lava by the slim light of a headlamp as camels carry camping gear.

Along the way, you'll smell sulfur and start to see smoke as the gleam of the cauldron of lava comes into view. This is one of few places in the world where you can stand on a volcanic crater rim and watch as seething molten rock cracks the slim gray surface of the lake and explodes into the night, casting a fiery glow against the caldera's shores. Spend the night watching the boiling molten rock before passing out in your tent, waking before dawn for another look, then walking back down in the rising light of morning.

WHAT YOU'LL SEE: Ethiopia's largest volcano (Erta Ale) | Lava lakes and fields | Boiling molten rock | Afar desert

POST-HIKE ACTIVITY

The Danakil Depression is known as one of the hottest, driest, and lowest places on Earth. Another must-see attraction is the area's intensely colorful hydrothermal fields, made by hot springs mixing with salt and mineral deposits, which creates the conditions for specialized, multicolored algae to grow.

A lava lake, dubbed the "gateway to hell," sits in the center of constantly active shield volcano Erta Ale.

TUGELA FALLS, THE DRAKENSBERG

The Roof of South Africa

DISTANCE: 8.7 miles (14 km) round-trip   **LENGTH OF TRIP:** 4 to 6 hours
BEST TIME TO GO: Austral fall   **DIFFICULTY:** Moderate

The Drakensberg, South Africa's most prominent mountain range, has a big personality with dramatic cliff faces, unpredictable weather, and swirling mists. Arguably the range's most famous geological feature is the Amphitheatre, a four-mile-long (6.5-km) escarpment that presides over the countryside. Hikers can get to the top in a day with a little muscle and nerve.

The trail starts at the Sentinel car park, zigzags up to a lookout, then traverses a steep mountainside. Banks of fog come and go, obscuring and revealing a landscape of dark cliffs, rust-colored mountainsides, and emerald slopes and valleys. Exposed rocky knobs require mindful footing, and a steep, narrow gully leads to the top of the escarpment, where the Tugela River flows like a silver thread through a landscape of exposed rock, sparse tufts of grass, and, at certain times of year, abundant yellow flowers. In the wet months, the river flows across the plateau and straight over the side, dropping more than half a mile (nearly a kilometer) down the cliffs below.

"I call it instant gratification," says Zimele "Zee" Ndaba, a certified hiking guide who works for nearby Witsieshoek Mountain Lodge. "You don't even have to work that hard and you come to the most beautiful-*est* of places."

WHAT YOU'LL SEE: Bushbucks I Baboons I Rock dassies I Otters I Duikers I Jackals

KNOW BEFORE YOU GO

Often, visitors take another route to descend from the plateau, which leads down a notch so steep it features a series of fixed chain ladders. For those with a fear of heights, you might consider forgoing the loop and instead retracing your steps.

Tugela is the world's second highest waterfall. The cascade drops a total of 3,110 feet (948 m) from the Drakensberg mountains.

INDIA VENSTER, TABLE MOUNTAIN

The End of a Continent

DISTANCE: About 1.6 miles (2.5 km) one way   **LENGTH OF TRIP:** 2.5 to 3.5 hours
BEST TIME TO GO: Austral summer   **DIFFICULTY:** Moderate

Flat-topped Table Mountain lords over the city of Cape Town like a supreme monarch. On its slopes, 65 hiking trails and more than 1,000 climbing routes beckon to the brave and energetic. Most visitors tromp up Platteklip Gorge, the easiest way up the mountain (not counting the cable car). But if you are not afraid of heights, arguably the most scenic and exciting path is the India Venster route, which starts at the outskirts of the city up the north side of the mountain through intimidating cliffs.

It can be very easy to get lost while scrambling through the jigsaw puzzle of cliffs, which is why it's wise to hire a guide for this route. Table Mountain's conditions also shouldn't be underestimated. It's known for the tablecloth-like clouds that unfurl over its edges, obscuring the peak for days at a time—and sometimes marooning climbers. But a jaunt up this highly variable route is also a fun, jungle-gym-like adventure.

Part of the unique allure of the India Venster route is that it traverses three sides of the peak, affording a panoply of shifting views, from the city of Cape Town to the glimmering sea and finally the rest of Table Mountain and the Cape Peninsula. At the top, the mountain has mercy on hikers' knees: Climbers can opt for the cable car to make the descent.

WHAT YOU'LL SEE: Orchids I King proteas I Rock hyraxes I Cape cobras I Sugarbirds

ALTERNATIVE ROUTE

For those who have a fear of heights or would prefer to climb the mountain without a guide, the Platteklip Gorge route up Table Mountain is the easiest, fastest, and most accessible trail. From the city avenues, it ascends the front—north—side of the mountain up steep rocks and ledges with a limited amount of scrambling.

Table Mountain overlooks Cape Town and Table Bay; its highest point is Maclear's Beacon at 3,563 feet (1,086 m).

PART FIVE

ASIA

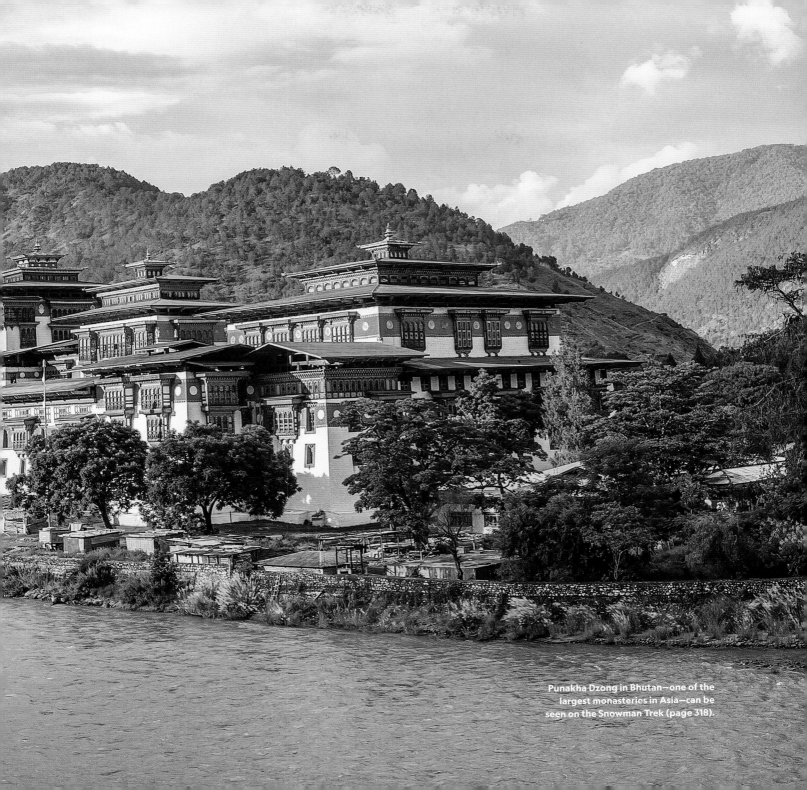

Punakha Dzong in Bhutan—one of the largest monasteries in Asia—can be seen on the Snowman Trek (page 318).

THE ISRAEL NATIONAL TRAIL

In the Footsteps of Prophets

DISTANCE: About 680 miles (1,100 km) one way   **LENGTH OF TRIP:** 8 to 10 weeks
BEST TIME TO GO: Spring and fall   **DIFFICULTY:** Moderate

For many of those who undertake the Israel National Trail, a long-distance path running the length of the country from north to south, the journey is more than a mere tour of ever changing landscapes. It's a deeply personal and spiritual pilgrimage in an ancestral homeland following in the footsteps of prophets. And for outdoorsy young Israelis, who make up the bulk of the trail's thru-hiking adherents, it's virtually a rite of passage. Many do it in groups and walk with an Israeli flag on their backpack, which often elicits words of encouragement from locals.

"The Israel Trail is unique in its spiritual, historical, and emotional dimension," says Aryeh Green, the author of *My Israel Trail: Finding Peace in the Promised Land,* a memoir about walking the trail after a difficult divorce. "That's not only true for Jews. You can be Christian or Muslim or atheist and still be incredibly moved by the historical references—like trekking through the Judean desert, which is where the prophets of Israel walked, where Jesus fled to and meditated in, and where King David fled from King Saul."

Starting near the border of Lebanon and Syria, the path veers south and west through lush forests to the Sea of Galilee and the Mediterranean coast, passes through outlying neighborhoods of Jerusalem, and plows south through the Negev to end at the resort town of Eilat on the Red Sea. Along the way, hikers stop to have coffee with Bedouin nomads, chat with farmers

CULTURAL IMMERSION

Trail angels—people who offer food, drink, and rides to thru-hikers—are a phenomenon on long treks. But Israeli trail angels are known to be particularly generous, going out of their way to offer rides and regularly hosting hikers in their homes, and providing food and showers.

OPPOSITE: The otherworldly Red Canyon in the Eilat Mountains has accessible hiking trails.

NEXT PAGES: Hikers cross underneath the Potash Conveyor Belt, which transports potash mined at Dead Sea factories to a cargo terminal in the Negev.

and shepherds in the countryside, and encounter other hikers along the trail. And they nearly trip over landmarks and ruins that clutter the landscape, from small, cast-aside items like ancient *gats*, or winemaking presses, to the tomb of Isaiah hidden in the woods, and the remnants of the ancient city of Zippori.

Most hikers travel in the fall or spring to avoid the high heat of summer, and many start in the northern region, which has more water. Walkers stroll through valleys patchworked with farms and lush forests that explode into bloom in spring. Stop to take a dip in a swimming hole, gaze over a sparkling lake from on high, inspect a wildflower, or savor berries or fruit, depending on the season.

The arid southern portions of the trail are also impressive in a different way. Here, the path launches off the edges of canyons, traipses across

WILDLIFE SPOTTING

While Israel may not be renowned as a Serengeti-like destination for wildlife-watching, thru-hikers commonly spot jackals, bobcats, snakes, and Nubian ibex. This ibex, adapted for hot, arid regions, frequents the Negev and Judean deserts and often ventures into hair-raisingly steep terrain to evade predators. Males feature long, slim, impressive horns.

gargantuan valleys, and sometimes even features ladders and rungs to help trekkers navigate the hazardous terrain. Large swaths of this desert are devoid of water sources and require caching water. You must also be aware of critters like scorpions and snakes that, while rare to spot, can be dangerous. But these lands also hold unexpected beauty, including expanses of earth cracked like pottery, colorful mineral deposits, and craters. Although the silence and emptiness of this monochrome of shifting beiges can seem forbidding, they also invite contemplation.

"Walking through that nothingness was probably the most powerful spiritual experience I had on the entire trek," says Green. "It takes all of the distractions of the world away, and you're left with you and the sky or you and God or you and the rest of humanity—or however you want to look at it."

ABOVE: Zippori National Park protects ancient relics, including ritual baths, a Jewish quarter, and the "Mona Lisa of the Galilee" mosaic.

OPPOSITE: Fishermen and surfers delight in the waters off Israel's beaches.

RICE TERRACES OF THE CORDILLERA

A 2,000-Year-Old Cultural Landscape

DISTANCE: Between 9 and 15 miles (15–24 km)   **LENGTH OF TRIP:** 5 to 8 hours
BEST TIME TO GO: Spring and fall   **DIFFICULTY:** Moderate

In the mountainous northern region of the island of Luzon, at least eight hours by car from Manila, the Ifugao, a minority ethnic group of people, have created a stunning cultural landscape over centuries. With basic tools of times past, they fashioned rice terraces that flow horizontally across lush hillsides in an attractive pattern of parallel lines. These rice terraces have survived for at least 2,000 years, and the best way to see them is as the locals do: on foot.

This one-day hike leads in a loop—between nine and 15 miles (15–24 km) round-trip, depending on the exact route taken—from the village of Hapao. As the terraces unfold before you, you might encounter women heading to market with produce, water buffalo plowing the fields, and men heaving stones to repair the terrace walls.

"Many are in awe at the scale and how the rice terraces continue to be worked," says Greg Hutchinson, founder of Tribal Adventures, which guides hiking trips in the area. "Hikers can roam freely, popping into homesteads to see rice being pounded in a giant wooden mortar and pestle, food being prepared, pigs fed, children playing games, reading books—and yes, communicating by Facebook with their friends."

WHAT YOU'LL SEE: Rice terraces **|** Water buffalo **|** Ifugao communities **|** Pigs **|** Chickens **|** Sweet potato fields

CULTURAL IMMERSION

The Ifugao are rice farmers who also grow sweet potatoes and raise livestock, like chicken and pigs, on their precipitous, stepped homelands. They typically live in settlements of five to 10 homes, many adorned with intricate carvings. Their religion is rich with deities, and they often host feasts and perform ceremonies in the gods' honor.

Sections of the Banaue Rice Terraces—made by the Ifugao people more than 2,000 years ago—are designated a UNESCO World Heritage site.

THE GREAT HIMALAYA TRAIL

The Ultimate Himalayan Epic

DISTANCE: About 1,050 miles (1,700 km) one way   **LENGTH OF TRIP:** 140 to 160 days
BEST TIME TO GO: Fall   **DIFFICULTY:** Expert-only

On long treks, life is distilled: Eat, sleep, walk. The challenge of pushing your body and navigating unfamiliar and difficult terrain can give rise to a stillness of mind that is hard to re-create in any other setting. The Great Himalaya Trail is arguably the consummate long trek. It's a stunner and a beast of a challenge, and few hikers emerge from the experience unchanged.

While the network of paths that forms the GHT loosely runs through Bhutan, India, Nepal, and Pakistan, the trail is most developed in Nepal, where it winds about 1,000 miles (1,600 km) from the Kanchenjunga region of the east to the Tibetan Plateau in the west, passing by every 26,300-foot (8,000-m) peak in the country and through the communities of at least a dozen unique mountain cultures. The often openhearted, friendly, hardworking residents profoundly touch trekkers as they walk through medieval villages, visit monasteries and temples, and observe Hindu, Buddhist, and animistic spiritual traditions. At times, the trail also leads up into the high country for weeks, higher than even the Nepalis live. This is where the elusive snow leopards reside.

Ann Price, the oldest woman to have completed the Nepali section of the Great Himalaya Trail, at age 65, set off on one of the first commercial trips with the outfitter World Expeditions in 2012. Within the first few weeks, she was struck by how removed she and her group were from the rest of the

CULTURAL IMMERSION

Yarsagumba, also known as Himalayan Viagra, is a caterpillar fungus that grows only in high-altitude areas of the Himalaya. It is valued as an aphrodisiac in China; this has spurred a massive business among harvesters, at once alleviating poverty for some families and depleting the natural supply.

OPPOSITE: Yak herders guide their livestock along a riverbed.

NEXT PAGES: The Great Himalaya Trail passes by each 26,247-foot (8,000-m) peak in Nepal and more than a dozen unique mountain communities.

WHAT YOU'LL SEE: Pine forests I Rhododendrons I Himalayan peaks I Medieval villages I Monasteries and temples I Yaks I Goats I Sheep

planet, the harshness of the conditions, and the mind-altering beauty of the mountains.

"It's not at all what a regular trekking trail would be," she says. "This is a mountaineering expedition . . . and the discomforts of what you are doing really start to sink in. There's no way out; no one's going to come and get you. You just have to dig deeper." Price recalls climbing over multiple 20,000-foot (6,000-m) passes, braving storms that waylaid her group for nearly a week, and the exhaustion of pounding the dirt for months at a time. She also remembers crossing raging rivers on nothing but a slippery, moss-covered log or a hair-raising suspension bridge, and climbing some 4,000 vertical feet (1,200 m) up a pass to camp in the snow. But the experience of threading through the highest mountains in the world—and feeling positively microscopic—was also remarkably transformative.

WILDLIFE SPOTTING

Other than the yaks, goats, and sheep of local residents, there isn't an abundance of wildlife in this harsh landscape. But with luck and patience, it's possible to spot giant vultures, colorful Nepali pheasants, and even a snow leopard or a rare red panda, a red-and-white, house cat–size mammal that lives in trees and is endangered by deforestation.

ABOVE: Nepali porters cross the turquoise Karnali River on an old suspension bridge.

OPPOSITE: Buddhist prayer flags, a common sight along the trail, are hung at Thorong La pass.

Trekkers traverse meadows freckled with wildflowers and fragrant old-growth forests of pine and rhododendron. Every day a new vista of gigantic, sparkling peaks comes into view. Occasionally, the route intersects with more trafficked hiking circuits like the trail around Annapurna, where you'll see other groups. In some of the more out-of-the-way villages, a trekking group is such an unusual spectacle that small mobs of children run out and greet you. Many hikers are struck by the kindness and compassion of the adults, too, who almost always welcome you with warmth and a smile. Come evening, when the temperature drops and you are ready to crawl into your cozy sleeping bag, take a moment to stop and look around—stars generously salt the sky and the moon illuminates the colossal faces of the world's highest peaks like a silvery kingdom. "Part of me didn't want to come back home," says Price. "It changes you."

AK-SUU TRAVERSE

The Great Peaks of Central Asia

DISTANCE: 71 miles (115 km) one way   **LENGTH OF TRIP:** 7 to 8 days
BEST TIME TO GO: Summer   **DIFFICULTY:** Strenuous

For many years, Kyrgyzstan was an unknown frontier for all except the most adventurous travelers. Thanks to a change in visa policies in the early 2010s and an increasing number of flights to the country, that is slowly changing. Visitors are discovering a nation rich in world-class mountain scenery and the colorful cultural traditions of alpine-dwelling nomads. In other words, it's a hiker's paradise.

One of the best multiday treks is the Ak-Suu Traverse, a challenging 71-mile (115-km) route that starts at the small village of Jyrgalan, an old coal-mining burg in the Ak-Suu District of Issyk-Kul that is transforming itself into an adventure-tourism hub. Over about a week, plow straight through the heart of Kyrgyzstan's beautiful high country, topping nine passes, enduring knee-bruising descents, all but tripping over abundant marmots, and tiptoeing across expansive valleys covered in loose rock.

From the high points, gaze over gargantuan glaciers that bulldoze down steep valleys and rows and rows of peaks, which stretch as far as the horizon. Hikers commonly encounter nomadic shepherds tending to their horses, sheep, goats, and cows, and, owing to a strong tradition of hospitality, it's not uncommon for trekkers to stay in nomads' tents and share *kumis,* a fermented horse milk drink. Come evening, camp by an emerald alpine lake and sink into sleep under a dome of stars.

WHAT YOU'LL SEE: Glaciers I Nomadic shepherds I Marmots I Horses I Sheep I Goats I Cows I Alpine lakes

HISTORICAL FOOTNOTE

Annexed by Russia in the 19th century, Kyrgyzstan was part of the U.S.S.R. during the Soviet era and declared its independence in 1991. The majority of the population is Kyrgyz, who are primarily Sunni Muslim and speak a Turkic-related language.

The Ak-Suu Traverse cuts through the heart of Kyrgyzstan's high country and across majestic valleys.

THE CHADAR TREK

A Frozen River, a Frozen Kingdom

DISTANCE: About 125 miles (200 km) round-trip **LENGTH OF TRIP:** 7 to 9 days
BEST TIME TO GO: Winter **DIFFICULTY:** Strenuous

During the winter, the people who live in the remote Zanskar Valley in the Indian Himalaya are cut off from other communities by the harsh weather and deep snows. The only way to get to Ladakh is by walking for days along the frozen Zanskar River, which snakes through a gorge that rises to a couple thousand feet (about 600 m) in some places and is colloquially known as India's Grand Canyon. A road is currently being constructed to connect Zanskar to the outside world, but what's known as the *chadar,* or frozen, trek remains. Locals continue to make the journey on the icy stream to shop, trade, work, or study in Ladakh, and travelers now come here in numbers to walk the storied route.

While the walking is flat and generally not technical, the trek requires fortitude to withstand the wintry conditions—temperatures often hover right around 0 degrees Fahrenheit (–20° to –15°C). For several days, hikers tramp through this tall, narrow hallway of stone, along a path of frozen water that changes from clear and blue to clouded with snow. On occasion, sections of the river have melted and you must either wade or climb up onto the cliffs to skirt around them. Crampons are usually not necessary, but large mukluk-like boots are recommended. Come evening, stay in tents next to the river or in caves where local people have taken shelter on this journey for many years. Since the route is a main thoroughfare, you

OPPOSITE: Built into the hills, the Lamayuru Monastery is the oldest in Ladakh—the first five temples were constructed in A.D. 1038.

NEXT PAGES: Chadar Trek porters make their way along the frozen Zanskar River.

will definitely walk alongside other hikers and locals.

"The local people, the Zanskaris—they're quite used to seeing foreigners walking by and are very hospitable," says Mandip Soin, the founder of Ibex Expeditions, an outfitter that pioneered the trek for visitors in the 1990s. "We have an interesting saying in India, which is *Athithi Devo Bhava,* or 'Guest Being God.' If you have a home and you have guests, then your home is blessed. People are very welcoming and chit-chatty."

Eventually, the gorge opens up into the spectacular Zanskar Valley itself, sparsely dotted with small communities, palaces, and monasteries built in styles reminiscent of Tibetan architecture. Stay in a Zanskari home in a village like Zangla, amble by the local nunnery, and soak in the daily life of these high-dwelling people, who go about their business with good humor in the crystalline air of the frigid Himalaya.

KNOW BEFORE YOU GO

The advent of trekking has brought livelihoods to local people, who are hired as guides and porters, but it has also changed the nature of the area. The local government has implemented a permit system that limits the number of visitors. Make sure to travel with a company that hires locals, packs out trash, and gives back to the community.

MOUNT RINJANI VOLCANO

A Sacred Volcano

DISTANCE: About 17 miles (27 km) one way
LENGTH OF TRIP: 2 to 4 days
BEST TIME TO GO: April through December
DIFFICULTY: Strenuous

Across the strait from Bali, the Indonesian island of Lombok is a hidden trove of lush mountain scenery and postcard-worthy beaches that are still being discovered by travelers. Over much of the island, the presence of one regal volcano, Rinjani, looms. It's so high that it creates its own weather system, which results in lush, fertile soil that nurtures plant life throughout the island. Rinjani is one of the most sacred volcanoes in Indonesia and plays host to a beautiful Hindu ceremony known as Mulang Pekelan, in which participants wear white prayer clothing, perform rituals, and toss gold, silver, and other valuables into the crater lake, Segara Anak.

Foreign trekkers also pilgrimage here to see Rinjani's unique caldera lake and summit. Although the climb is not technical, it does require a considerable level of fitness. Trails lead to the 12,224-foot (3,730-m) peak from the communities of Senaru and Sembalun, and most hikers take three or four days to travel from one town to the summit, then down to the other.

The most common route starts in Senaru because the first day, which includes more than 6,000 feet (2,000 m) of elevation gain, is shaded by jungle. The terrain varies along the way as you walk through different ecosystems, from forest haunted by monkeys and birds to open grasslands.

Camp on the rim of the crater, which has views down to the aquamarine water—warm and swimmable thanks to geothermal heating—and a volcanic

OPPOSITE: **Stand above the clouds on the peak of Mount Rinjani (12,224 feet/3,726 m).**

NEXT PAGES: **Smoke spills from Mount Rinjani as it erupts just before dusk.**

cone that was formed in the mid-1990s and regularly breathes plumes of smoke like a cigar-puffing uncle.

On summit day, hikers wake before dawn to climb more than 5,000 vertical feet (1,500 m) through the dark to the summit to watch the sun rise over the island and the sea. In the soft light, it's not hard to imagine why locals have long thought of this place as spiritual. If it's clear, views extend over Bali's Mount Agung, another sacred active volcano, and the Gili Islands.

"Some of my favorite things are being on the crater rim and watching the clouds roll up the valley and fill the caldera," says Angus Lawrence, founder of Rinjani Dawn Adventures, an outfitter that guides the climb. "As day gives way to night, the sky comes alive with the spiraling majesty of the Milky Way. Climbing Mount Rinjani is far more than reaching the summit—it's about reconnecting with a living planet."

HISTORICAL FOOTNOTE

An ancient volcano known as Samalas once stood in the general area where Mount Rinjani stands today. In 1257, it exploded in a mega-eruption, tossing as much as 10 cubic miles (42 cu km) of rock and ash into the air, blocking sunlight and cooling the planet worldwide, possibly for as long as the rest of the century.

SIX WATERFALLS HIKE

An Empire of Waterfalls

DISTANCE: 3.2 miles (5.1 km) round-trip   **LENGTH OF TRIP:** 5 to 7 hours
BEST TIME TO GO: Year-round   **DIFFICULTY:** Moderate

Thanks to an extraordinary amount of rainfall and steep topography, the island of Pohnpei in Micronesia is alive with waterfalls. Rivers spill out of gorges at seemingly every turn, and the sounds of rushing water fill the rainforests. For waterfall fans, the Six Waterfalls Hike is the equivalent of an all-star game. The route starts in the forest on a narrow track, slippery with tree roots. The first waterfall, Pahnairlap, comes into earshot within an hour of hiking—you'll hear its rumble before you feel its spray and see it tumble magnificently, framed by dark rock and a mop of lush greenery.

From there, the route leads through forest but mostly along—and more often *in*—the Lehnmesi River. Waterfalls then start to appear more regularly, resplendent in their diverse glory, from small cascades dropping into serene pools to long, statuesque stunners. The sixth falls, Lipwentiak, is also hidden from view. Hikers can choose to clamber over rocky outcroppings or simply stash their backpacks and swim the slot between rocks up to the waterfall, which pours out of a cleft into a wide, generous pool. Deep in the jungle, with no one else around, it can feel as if you were the first person to discover it.

WHAT YOU'LL SEE: Waterfalls I Lehnmesi River I Jungle I Fantails I Pohnpei flycatchers I Long-billed white-eyes

POST-HIKE ACTIVITY

Offshore of Pohnpei, the blocky stone ruins of the ancient city of Nan Madol, built between 1200 and 1500, rise out of the sea. Known as the "Venice of the Pacific," they consist of more than 100 man-made islands topped with palaces, tombs, and temples of coral and basalt boulders. No one knows just how the ancients built this ceremonial center.

Kepirohi Waterfall—66 feet (20 m) tall and 98 feet (30 m) wide—cascades down basalt rock into a shallow pool that is perfect for swimming.

SNOWMAN TREK

One of the World's Most Fearsome Treks

DISTANCE: About 190 miles (300 km) one way **LENGTH OF TRIP:** 25 to 30 days
BEST TIME TO GO: Early fall   **DIFFICULTY:** Expert-only

Among the Himalayan countries, Bhutan holds an especially alluring mystique. Relatively small, the country fiercely guards its Buddhist culture and limits the number of its visitors. Even though its peaks are smaller than Nepal's, Bhutan's Snowman Trek has a reputation for being the world's most challenging multiday hike. While there's room for debate, it's certainly a serious undertaking. The route encompasses nearly 200 miles (320 km) of high, remote, rugged, Himalayan territory, crossing 11 high passes—with a couple 17,000-footers (5,000-m) thrown in for good measure—as it traces the country's northern border, from the Paro Valley to the remote eastern region of Bumthang. Many trekkers do not complete the trip because of the terrain, the altitude, and the tricky calculus of the weather, which ranges from intense high-altitude sun to ferocious snowstorms.

For those whom the mountains let pass, there are untold wonders in these hidden aeries. Pass through sprawling meadows that come alive with small flowers when the snows thaw. Travel through thick forests of pine and rhododendron. Look up at the cliffs for blue sheep and even higher for the enormous lammergeier. Glaciers and their work, from moraines to milky-blue alpine lakes, dot the landscape. And at seemingly every turn, peaks, such as Chomolhari and Jichu Drake, shadow the valleys like benevolent uncles. But it's the friendly outlook of the residents that usually touches visitors most deeply.

WILDLIFE SPOTTING

Snow leopards frequent the high, remote slopes of Bhutan's Himalaya but are seen only occasionally. These seven-foot-long (2-m) creatures are active at dusk and dawn, hunting wild sheep, ibex, and other mammals, and typically live in solitude. Their large paws allow them to travel across deep snow, and their long tails help them balance in uneven terrain.

OPPOSITE: Paro Taktsang Monastery was built around the Taktsang Senge Samdup cave, where Buddhists have visited since the eighth century.

NEXT PAGES: Glacier views—and grazing horses—await outside your tent in Narethang.

Hikers commonly meet yak herders who walk the pastures with their livestock. Near villages of tidy stone houses, farmers thresh wheat and schoolchildren sing and play. Around the distinctive white edifices of *dzongs,* monks engage in their daily tasks. The care and presence of the mountains' residents, mixed with the beautiful harshness of the terrain, can work on visitors in mysterious ways—physical, emotional, and spiritual. As opposed to an accomplishment of willpower, it can feel as if a successful trek is granted by the grace of the mountains themselves.

"The expansive and beautiful scenery—and lack of a connection to the outside world—plunges the trekker entirely into the present moment," says Kevin Grange, author of the hiking memoir *Beneath Blossom Rain: Discovering Bhutan on the Toughest Trek in the World*. "Every sight, sound and image pulses with a kind of sacredness, relevance, and meaning."

CULTURAL IMMERSION

The majority of Bhutanese are Buddhist and the trappings of the religion permeate the country's culture, from prayer flags strung from hilltop shrines to monasteries, such as the famed cliffside Paro Taktsang, also known as the Tiger's Nest, and the impressive *dzong* at Punakha. If you're lucky, you might overhear the monks chanting.

LAOZHAI MOUNTAIN

A Land of Giant Thumbs

DISTANCE: Less than 1.5 miles (2.5 km) round-trip   **LENGTH OF TRIP:** 1 to 1.5 hours
BEST TIME TO GO: Spring and fall   **DIFFICULTY:** Moderate

The striking hills of the Chinese region of Guangxi have long been known as an inspiration for writers and artists. Giant limestone karsts spike out of a landscape quilted with lush chartreuse and emerald fields, threaded by the Li River. The area is now a hub for outdoor activities, and many travelers sail through the countryside on bicycles, rock climb the precipitous faces of the karsts, and kayak the river. Hikes tend to come in two varieties: straight up or bone flat. Laozhai Mountain, which rises from the historic village of Xingping, falls into the former category—it's short and fierce with a brilliant payoff at the end.

From the village of Xingping, hikers plow upward, climbing sections with steep ladder-like steps. In certain areas, you might need to negotiate some loose rocks as you StairMaster your way up the forest-clothed slope. At the top, gaze over a splendid view of rectilinear rice paddies, clusters of Monopoly-like homes and hotels, and the Li dotted with boats that appear as small as toys. If you brought a headlamp to aid your journey back, stay for sunset, when the waning sunlight tints the sky hues of orange as rows of karsts recede in the hazy distance.

WHAT YOU'LL SEE: Limestone karsts I Li River I Historic Xingping village I Rectilinear rice paddies

ALTERNATIVE ROUTE

Moon Hill, with its crescent-shaped natural arch, is a renowned landmark near the town of Yangshuo. The hike leads up about 800 steps through lush stands of bamboo to the arch, which frames views of the surrounding countryside. A small path near the top veers off—follow it for vistas from the very top of the hill.

The ancient fishing village of Xingping sits along the Li River, beneath Laozhai Mountain.

THE GREAT WALL OF CHINA

China's Great Masterwork

DISTANCE: 8.7 miles (14 km) one way   **LENGTH OF TRIP:** 6 to 8 hours
BEST TIME TO GO: Spring and fall   **DIFFICULTY:** Strenuous

Between the third century B.C. and the 17th century A.D., generations of workers constructed one of the most astonishing feats of engineering in human history: the Great Wall of China. In its entirety, it zigzagged more than 12,500 miles (20,000 km), encompassing disparate (and sometimes parallel) lengths of wall, as well as towers, shelters, passes, bridges, and forts. Many sections still exist today. To gain an appreciation of the structure that protected empires, consider walking one of the less frequented areas, such as Jinshanling, a well-preserved section, and Gubeikou, an untouched section from the Ming dynasty that is located almost 90 miles (140 km) northeast of Beijing.

Here, the wall is built of stone and rises 23 feet (7 m) tall and 20 feet (6 m) wide. Every 330 feet (100 m), watchtowers—which were used as forts, to store supplies, and as sleeping quarters for soldiers—rise up out of the edifice, which snakes through the hills. The topography is steep, which means that hiking is strenuous. It's best to undertake the walk in the spring or fall—summer can be intensely hot and humid and winters cold and snowy. In areas where the wall is crumbling, walkers must negotiate loose, slippery stones. But the vertical gain and loss allow brilliant views of the wall as it winds through the countryside.

"When you walk on this part of the wall, you can touch the centuries-old watchtowers and enjoy the beautiful scenery from both China and Mongol

OPPOSITE: Legend holds that when couples leave a lock along the Great Wall their love will last an eternity.

NEXT PAGES: It is estimated that there are more than 10,000 watchtowers set along the Great Wall.

sides—all in China now," says Gary Lee, founder of Great Wall Hiking, which guides hikes along many sections of the wall. "It's almost as if you could see the marching Mongolian army."

Explore the wall for evocative hints to what the past might have been like—see where soldiers kept watch, slept, and shot arrows from on high. Some of the bricks have inscriptions that catalog where and when they were made, reminding modern viewers that this ancient structure was all built by hand.

During the softly glowing hours of sunset and sunrise, the landscape takes on an almost mystical quality. It's easy to imagine what it might have been like to see the Great Wall of China hundreds of years ago when it acted as a strategic military barrier. Its bulk and fortitude suggest the depth of intelligence that fueled this great civilization—and is no less mind-boggling today than it was when it was first built.

KNOW BEFORE YOU GO

To support the livelihoods of local people, consider eating meals in nearby restaurants and staying the night in a guesthouse instead of heading straight back to Beijing. Some locals will also guide you in areas where the wall is crumbling and you must traverse farmers' fields and brushy areas.

TIGER LEAPING GORGE

China's Great Chasm

DISTANCE: **16 miles (26 km) one way**   **LENGTH OF TRIP:** **2 to 3 days**
BEST TIME TO GO: **Winter**   **DIFFICULTY:** **Strenuous**

O nce upon a time, a hunter chased a tiger through a gorge in western China, eventually trapping it. To escape, the feline jumped daringly across the canyon at its narrowest point—about 80 feet (24 m). This is the legend behind how Tiger Leaping Gorge received its name.

Today, travelers come to see dazzling views of this steep-walled mountain chasm, carved out by the roaring Jinsha River. Most hikers tackle the 16-mile (26-km) upper trail in two days, starting from the hamlet of Qiaotou and staying in one of several guesthouses that dot the path. The rocky trail has no shortage of drama, from its infamous 28 bends, which wind some 1,500 vertical feet (450 m) up from the Naxi Guesthouse, a favorite stop among hikers, to steep cliffs and waterfalls that trickle or tumble over the path. Along the way, local Naxi people, a minority group, tend herds of goats, cows, and horses that trot down the trail. Above, Jade Dragon Snow Mountain and the Haba Snow Mountain rear their jagged heads. As you walk, breathe in the clear air and take in the tableau of forests, sky, and clouds. If you're lucky, you'll spot rainbows flashing and disappearing, and clouds that shift and move, clinging delicately to the dramatic slopes like lace.

WHAT YOU'LL SEE: Jinsha River | Waterfalls | Goats | Cows | Horses | Rainbows

CULTURAL IMMERSION

The Naxi speak a Tibeto-Burman language, and, despite vast changes in China in the 20th century, some still maintain traditional matriarchal family structures. Their religion, Dongba, is shamanistic and related to Tibetan Buddhism. In China, they live mainly in Yunnan and Sichuan Provinces and grow crops such as rice, corn, and potatoes.

One of the deepest gorges in the world, Tiger Leaping Gorge offers stunning water views amid ragged stone cliffs.

GOTEMBA TRAIL, MOUNT FUJI

The Emblem of Japan

DISTANCE: About 10 miles (16 km) round-trip   **LENGTH OF TRIP:** 2 days
BEST TIME TO GO: Late summer   **DIFFICULTY:** Strenuous

The unmistakable cone-shaped form of 12,388-foot (3,776-m) Mount Fuji is a symbol of Japan and is firmly lodged in the national consciousness. The tallest peak in the country, it sits about 60 miles (100 km) southwest of Tokyo and for centuries has inspired spiritual pilgrimages and works of art and poetry. Temples, shrines, and lodgings for pilgrims dot its slopes, and people come in the hundreds of thousands to climb up the sacred peak, oftentimes in the dark of predawn to watch the sunrise from the top. (And mostly during the official summer climbing season.) Although it hasn't erupted since 1707, Fuji is still considered an active volcano and features the telltale signs, such as lava caves, hot springs, and volcanic vents.

While it is well loved, Fuji's hiking trails are not for couch potatoes. (It's common for hikers to buy a Mount Fuji walking stick to help them reach the top—and also to keep as a souvenir.) Four trails lead to the summit and each climbs more than 4,000 vertical feet (1,200 m). Yoshida is the easiest and most popular, and buses travel directly from Tokyo to deposit peak baggers right at the trailhead. (Hiking with so many other summit-seekers is a cultural experience, but be prepared to travel at the pace of the line.) The Gotemba Trail, by contrast, starts a bit lower than the others, features fewer shops and facilities along the way, and hosts the fewest travelers. From

OPPOSITE: Snowcapped Mount Fuji looms large above Lake Ashi and its surrounding forest.

NEXT PAGES: Trekkers make their way through a fog-laden forest at the base of Mount Fuji.

about 4,600 feet (1,400 m), make your way up switchbacks in a moonscape of black volcanic sand. Partway up, several mountain huts house hikers looking to rest before a sunrise summit bid. The next morning, join the line of snaking headlamps up the trail.

Waiting for the moment when the sun crests the horizon is a cherished tradition, and you will be joined by hundreds, if not thousands, of other people doing the same thing. Watch as the glow of morning strengthens, the sky dyes itself orange and red, and eventually the great star appears on the eastern horizon to a spectacle of camera flashes. On the way back down, the Gotemba Trail follows the same route as the ascent, then peels off to an area with soft sandy sections known as *osunabashiri,* where you can careen down the steep slope with unadulterated glee, the countryside of Japan spread out magnificently beneath you.

HISTORICAL FOOTNOTE

Since the 14th century, Mount Fuji, also known as Fujisan, has inspired paintings, poems, garden design, and many other works of art and literature. In the 19th century, artist Katsushika Hokusai's wood-block prints influenced Western artists and helped establish the mountain as a symbol of Japan beyond its borders, too.

THE JORDAN TRAIL

Civilizations Past and Present

DISTANCE: About 400 miles (650 km) one way   **LENGTH OF TRIP:** 30 to 40 days
BEST TIME TO GO: Spring and fall   **DIFFICULTY:** Strenuous

I n the 2010s, a spate of long-distance trails emerged around the world, many designed as a means of bringing sustainable tourism development to remote, rural communities. Among them, the Jordan Trail is a standout. Few long trails more skillfully combine the beauty of the scenery, the country's deep archaeological heritage, and the richness of its contemporary culture. The Jordan Trail, which officially opened to visitors in 2017, leads from the shores of the Red Sea across the sands and ridges of Wadi Rum, by the famed ancient city of Petra, and through the forested hills of the north, all while passing more than 50 local communities along the way.

Many of these footpaths are not new. For centuries, human beings have traveled these lands with their herds or for trade, from the Moabites, Edomites, and Ammonites to the Romans in the early centuries of the first millennium A.D. Many modern-day hikers don't tackle the entirety of the trail, but rather tick off sections of it, such as the 80-mile (129-km) route that connects Wadi Rum with Petra, the ancient caravan city, one of the longest stretches of wilderness on the whole path. Here, marvel at the mind-clearing emptiness of huge stretches of sand, gigantic wadis, and imposing buttes. Come nighttime, stare up into an inky-black sky, freckled with stars, and savor the undisturbed stillness and silence of the desert.

OPPOSITE: Wadi Rum protects 278 square miles (720 sq km) of desert wilderness, including huge sandstone and granite mountains.

NEXT PAGES: Candles cast their glow on the Treasury at Petra, a UNESCO World Heritage site.

WHAT YOU'LL SEE: Red Sea I Wadi Rum I Petra I Gigantic wadis I Olive groves I Orchards I Artisan crafts I Crusaders' castle

Farther north, the landscape shifts into a mosaic of ecosystems, from mountaintops to farmlands. And on the northernmost section, between the castle of Aljoun and Um Qais, travelers walk through olive groves and orchards, and often stay with local families who have developed a series of homestays and offer meals and artisan crafts.

Flanking the western edge of Jordan, the trail on the whole is mesmerizing for the number of ruins and communities along the way. Some hikers even spot potsherds and ancient tools lying trailside. In Petra, imagine what it might have been like to gaze up at the regal edifices, partly carved into the rock, during Nabataean or Roman times. At Kerak, a crusader's castle, bring a flashlight to explore the shadowed stone passages of a structure that dates to the 12th century—but acted as a fortress since biblical times. And in the ancient agricultural city of Al-Salt, wander through mazes of yellow sandstone buildings, along narrow winding streets, where people have lived and traded for centuries.

CULTURAL IMMERSION

While many Jordanians speak English, you will be well received if you learn some words and phrases in Arabic. When approaching Bedouin camps, call out and approach from the left, the men's side. If there are only women in the camp, have the women in your group approach them.

BHABHA PASS TREK

From a Hindu Enclave to a Buddhist Valley

DISTANCE: About 32 miles (52 km) one way   **LENGTH OF TRIP:** 5 to 6 days
BEST TIME TO GO: Fall   **DIFFICULTY:** Moderate

Sitting in the northern reaches of India, Himachal Pradesh is a repository of scenic beauty, from high Himalayan peaks and deeply incised gorges to terraced slopes and dense forests—in other words, a trekker's nirvana. Among many possible routes, the Bhabha Pass trek is unique in the diversity of its terrain and local culture as you walk from a predominantly Hindu area to a land inhabited by Buddhists.

From Kafnu, hikers travel through meadows and pine, oak, and birch forests. Above high grasslands, bedecked with wild blooms, loom the toothy faces of mountains like 17,191-foot (5,240-m) Hansbeshan, 21,320-foot (6,500-m) Kinnaur Kailash, and 20,401-foot (6,220-m) Indrasan Peak. The highest point of the route is the Bhabha Pass itself, which tops 14,763 feet (4,500 m) and is snowbound most of the year.

"The day you are crossing the pass, you say why did I do this?" says Rajesh Ojha, co-founder of Banjara Camps & Retreats, an outfitter that guides hikers on the pass. "But the overall experience of the trek is fascinating—the landscape changes, the religion changes, the rituals all change."

As you descend, negotiate the rubble of glacial moraines, soak in the kaleidoscopic colors of this dry, rocky land, and emerge from the wilderness at Mudh, a picturesque collection of whitewashed Tibetan-style homes perched on an arid hillside in the Spiti Valley.

WHAT YOU'LL SEE: Meadows I Pine and birch forests I Grasslands I Wildflowers I Tibetan-style homes I Glacial moraines

POST-HIKE ACTIVITY

The Spiti Valley, with its lunar landscapes and communities of white homes, deserves time for exploration. Kaza, situated on the Spiti River, is the largest settlement, and Key is a particularly notable sight. A prim, attractive monastery, perched on a knob, it overlooks a patchwork of green fields and a colossal valley guarded by peaks.

Himachal Pradesh's Pin Valley National Park protects snow leopards and Siberian ibex, as well as a few small mountainside villages.

THE JIRISAN RIDGE

A Sacred Mountain Landscape

DISTANCE: 37 miles (60 km) one way   **LENGTH OF TRIP:** 2 to 4 days
BEST TIME TO GO: Spring and fall   **DIFFICULTY:** Moderate

For many Koreans, the mountains of Jirisan National Park in the very southern part of the peninsula are considered spiritual and sacred. Legend has it that fools can come to these peaks and become wise from contact with their transcendent beauty. As a result, crowds of Koreans venture to this national park, seeking an immersion in its forests, which are illuminated by blooms in spring and spectacular reds, oranges, and golds in fall. Numerous hiking trails thread through the mountains, lead to rolling waterfalls, and top out on the ridges. The most epic of them all is Jirisan Ridge.

There are several different variations of the trail along the ridge, but many hikers tackle the 37-mile (59-km) route from the Hwaeomsa Temple in the east to Daewonsa Temple in the west. Five shelters along the way house hikers in sardine-can-like bunks (reserve your spot well ahead of time) and offer basic snacks like ramen (but you are well advised to bring most of your own food and a cook set).

The route leads along stone-and-dirt paths through peaceful tunnels of trees and pokes up onto ridges with views over softly undulating mountains. Many hikers make a point of reaching Cheonwangbong Peak at sunrise. Watch and listen to the murmurings of other reverent summiteers as sunlight graces the sky over this peaceful sanctuary.

WHAT YOU'LL SEE: Waterfalls I Temples I Asiatic black bears I Korean winter hazel trees I Water deer

WILDLIFE SPOTTING

Asiatic black bears were once quite rare in Jirisan National Park, but, thanks to a restoration project, they are growing in number. These black- or brown-coated bears have a striking white, crescent-shaped patch of fur on their chests. They eat fruit, nuts, insects, small animals, carrion, and the occasional beehive.

A wooden path, draped in fall foliage, leads the way to Baemsagol Valley in Jirisan National Park.

THE GREAT BAIKAL TRAIL

The World's Oldest, Deepest Lake

DISTANCE: 36 miles (58 km) one way **LENGTH OF TRIP: 3 to 4 days**
BEST TIME TO GO: Summer **DIFFICULTY: Moderate**

For decades, Russian conservationists, nature lovers, and hikers dreamed of a trail that would circumnavigate Lake Baikal, the oldest and deepest lake in the world, stretching 395 miles (636 km) long in southeastern Siberia. In 2003, the dream started to materialize when the first teams of volunteers arrived to build footpaths. Every year since, these hardy bands of devotees continue to build the trail, which now totals about 310 miles (500 km) in segments all around the lake.

One of the most easily accessible sections runs 36 miles (58 km) along the lakeshore from Listvyanka, a quirky resort town, to the community of Bolshoye Goloustnoye, where you can catch a bus back to the city of Irkutsk. On this stretch, most hikers camp for several nights and spend one evening in the very small, serene, former mining community of Bolshie Koty, which is only reachable by foot or boat. (There are no restaurants or hotels but some locals open their homes to hikers.) The trail winds through cool, fragrant, evergreen forests; climbs up and behind cliffs; and traverses the rugged shoreline. Keep an eye out for dwarf lilies, striking orange globeflowers, and rabbit's cabbage, a cactus-like alpine succulent. Ultimately, the lake itself, by virtue of its beauty and immensity, is what truly captures the imagination.

WHAT YOU'LL SEE: Evergreen forests I Dwarf lilies I Globeflowers I Alpine succulents

POST-HIKE ACTIVITY

Bolshoye Goloustnoye is a pleasant place to spend a few hours. Check out the photogenic church dedicated to St. Nicholas, which sits on the shores of the lake. From the outskirts of town, a 1.8-mile (3-km) trail heads up to the top of a holy mountain and affords views over the river valley, lake, and village.

Gaze at snowcapped peaks in the distance as you walk across Lake Baikal's sandy shore.

MOUNT EVEREST BASE CAMP

Glimpsing the Top of the World

DISTANCE: About 80 miles (130 km) round-trip **LENGTH OF TRIP:** 14-plus days
BEST TIME TO GO: Spring, summer, and fall **DIFFICULTY:** Strenuous

Even for high-dwelling people from other regions, the Himalaya give the term "mountain" a whole other meaning. These gargantuan peaks seem to be on a different scale than many of the other great mountain ranges of the world. They're the equivalent of mountain royalty, and the queen of them all is Everest herself, the highest peak on Earth at 29,035 feet (8,850 m).

First climbed by Tenzing Norgay and Edmund Hillary in 1953, Everest now attracts hundreds of climbers annually (often paying upwards of $50,000 for a guided expedition). But one needn't attempt a summit bid to catch a glimpse of this legendary peak, known in Sanskrit as *Sagarmatha* or "Peak of Heaven" and in one Tibetan language as *Chomolungma* or "Goddess Mother of the World." Many hikers take base camp itself as their goal.

"It's one of my favorite experiences traveling anywhere," says Justin Wood, who manages trips and operations for REI Adventures globally, including the trek to Everest Base Camp. "Anyone who enjoys climbing at any level can't help but be completely awed by Everest in real life. And the thing that makes this trek so powerful and unforgettable is you layer onto it trekking through amazing villages that have never had roads and have always only been accessed on foot." The Everest region is largely inhabited by the Sherpa people, who originally hail from eastern Tibet and maintain a rich Buddhist and animistic culture.

CULTURAL IMMERSION

Shops and lodges dot the route to Everest Base Camp, which means that many Western snacks like chips and candy bars are available (often at a considerable price). But regional foods are also in plentiful supply, the most common being *dal bhat,* a filling and nutritious dish of steamed rice and lentil soup.

OPPOSITE: Thousands of trekkers make their way to Everest Base Camp every year.

NEXT PAGES: A stone path leads to the entrance of Namche Bazaar, the staging point for most expeditions to Everest and home of most Sherpas.

WHAT YOU'LL SEE: Dudh Kosi River I Sagarmatha National Park I Namche Bazaar I Tengboche Monastery I Yaks I Everest climbers

They have also long acted as guides and porters for trekkers shooting for Everest.

The trek to base camp starts from Lukla, where a short, hair-raising runway welcomes trekkers in tiny planes. Typically, hikers leave the same day, descending to the Dudh Kosi River then heading through rolling terrain to Phakding, a nice overnight stopping point. The next day, they pass the entrance of Sagarmatha National Park and head uphill to Namche Bazaar, a colorful market town and staging point for mountaineering expeditions in the area. In the coming days, the area's high peaks come into view: Nuptse, Lhotse, Ama Dablam, and Everest. Locals believe that these mountains are the abodes of the gods, and it's not hard to imagine why when staring up at their mind-blowing bulk.

As the days unfold, the terrain rolls higher and higher as you pass remote shrines festooned with prayer flags, the Tengboche Monastery beneath

KNOW BEFORE YOU GO

The weather can be unpredictable in this kingdom of Nepalese peaks, which means an array of layers is critical. But one condition that sometimes catches hikers off guard is the strong high-altitude sun. Be sure to bring plenty of sunscreen and a broad-brimmed hat, since UV rays are stronger at altitude and can reflect off snow.

the shadow of Ama Dablam, and countryside tinkling with yak bells. Typically, trekkers stay in mountain lodges and teahouses along the way and take rest days to safely acclimatize themselves to the oxygen-poor conditions of the high peaks. (Give yourself at least 14 days so that there's plenty of time to adapt.) Because the trek is so popular, evenings are often spent chatting with a diverse international crowd of travelers, rehashing the day's adventures.

When Everest climbers are in base camp, conscientious tour operators offer them plenty of space. A great spot to take in the action is from Kala Patar, a nearby peak that, at over 18,000 feet (about 5,500 m), has unobstructed views of Everest and base camp. During summit season, in late spring, a tapestry of colorful tents spreads out below. Head up Kala Patar at sunrise to see this goddess of the world radiate with soft pink-orange alpenglow.

DOI LUANG CHIANG DAO

A Gem Among Northern Thailand's Peaks

DISTANCE: About 10.5 miles (17 km) round-trip **LENGTH OF TRIP:** 1 to 2 days
BEST TIME TO GO: November through February **DIFFICULTY:** Strenuous

Unbeknownst to many of Thailand's droves of beach-seeking visitors, the northern regions of the country are rippling with forest-clad mountains and play host to some of the best hikes in Southeast Asia. Watching the sunrise and sunset on some of the more popular summits is a hallowed rite for many domestic travelers, and one great viewing spot is Doi Luang Chiang Dao.

The thigh-burning hike to the top, at 7,300 feet (2,225 m) weeds out some of the masses that visit other peaks, and its diversity in elevation makes ideal habitats for unusual plants, such as rare orchid species and an endemic palm tree. Pass through evergreen forests up to a high valley, where limestone crags pop up all around. "The view keeps changing as you make your way to the summit," says Malee Keratitaweesuk, owner of Malee's Nature Lovers Bungalows, which sits at the peak's base and guides hikers to the top. "The landscape and nature are amazing—and the overnighters get surprised by the chilly nights!" The vistas of raggedy peaks will surely capture your attention, but keep an eye out for smaller wonders, too, such as the rare gorals—goatlike ungulates—that call this peak home.

WHAT YOU'LL SEE: Orchids I Palm trees I Evergreen forests I Limestone crags I Gorals I Remarkable sunrises and sunsets

ALTERNATIVE ROUTE

The mountainous area of northern Thailand around the city of Chiang Rai features numerous hikes. One unique, very short option is Phu Chi Fa, a favorite among Thai tourists. In the pre-dawn hours, hikers schlep about 20 minutes from the parking area to the peak to watch the sunrise over a mountain-fringed valley, paved with cobblestone clouds.

Arrive at the top of Doi Luang Chiang Dao before sunset to take in the arresting views.

SA PA HILL STATION

Rice Terraces, Forests, and Hill Tribes

DISTANCE: 7 to 10 miles (11–16 km) round-trip **LENGTH OF TRIP:** 5 to 6 hours
BEST TIME TO GO: March through May; September through November **DIFFICULTY:** Moderate

Sa Pa, a hill station established by the French in 1922 in northwest Vietnam, is the country's trekking hub. The town itself is a colorful gathering place for the hill tribes that live in the region (and the hub of a bustling tourist industry), but it's perhaps best known for what lies beyond it: steep valleys stair-stepped with vibrant rice terraces, dripping forests, pint-size villages, and cool mists that breeze in and out, lending the whole landscape a mystical air.

Several hill tribes live here, including the Black Hmong, the Red Dzao, the Tay, the Giáy, the Thai, and the Phù Lá. Many individuals offer guiding services, homestays, and home-cooked meals with heaps of tofu, pork, rice, and local vegetables.

Numerous trails link the local communities, but there aren't generally designated hiking routes or trails—hikers simply meander and loop around. That's a large part of the reason that it's useful to have a knowledgeable guide. One local service, Sapa Sisters Trekking Adventures, works to empower local Hmong women by training and employing them as guides. Follow one of the women as she leads you through the high mountains, ravines, and rice terraces around Sa Pa. Frequently, rain will come by—a free shower, some might say—and bathe the verdant land that births these lush fields, forests, and paddies.

WHAT YOU'LL SEE: Black Hmong, Red Dzao, Tay, Giáy, Thai, and Phù Lá hill tribes | Rice terraces | Ravines | Forests

POST-HIKE ACTIVITY

The culturally rich area of Sa Pa has much to offer beyond hiking. Peruse a market where locals come to swap goods and produce. Some local outfitters offer classes in Hmong batik and even Hmong cooking classes, where students can learn how to make dishes like Vietnamese pancakes and fried banana cakes.

Northwest of Hanoi, the small mountain town of Sa Pa sits at 5,249 feet (1,600 m) above sea level.

PART SIX

OCEANIA, AUSTRALIA, AND ANTARCTICA

Nikau palm trees line the Heaphy
Track (page 356) in Kahurangi
National Park, New Zealand.

THE HEAPHY TRACK

From Mountains to the Coast

DISTANCE: 49 miles (78 km) one way   **LENGTH OF TRIP: 4 to 6 days**
BEST TIME TO GO: Austral spring through fall   **DIFFICULTY: Moderate**

Since at least the 14th century, Maori occupied and traveled through the area that is now known as Kahurangi National Park. Many were on their way to look for *pounamu,* a prized greenish stone that they used to make weapons, tools, and artwork. Today, people come to Kahurangi seeking treasures of a different sort—thick stands of unusual palms, expansive green valleys filled with tussocks, and the roaring surf of the empty coast.

Because it is somewhat hard to get to and requires a car shuttle, the Heaphy Track is not as frequented as some of New Zealand's other "Great Walks," a collection of primo trails maintained by the Department of Conservation. But, luckily, several huts punctuate the trail, and, at least in the evenings, you might cook a pot of grub and chat with Kiwis or international visitors who are doing the same. Because the trail is not terribly strenuous in terms of elevation gain, intrepid families with children often undertake it.

The scenery changes to a remarkable degree as the trail wends from forested mountainous areas down to the coast, studded with beaches and cliffs. Pass through valleys filled with the long, swaying grasses of tussocks. Tromp through mossy beech forests that are so green and magical that some call them enchanted, and keep an eye out for hidden limestone caves that snake underground. Eventually, hikers encounter stands of striking nikau palms,

OPPOSITE: A suspension bridge hovers over the Kohaihai River in Kahurangi National Park.

NEXT PAGES: South Island edelweiss alpine flowers bloom with woolly white bracts.

which give the landscape a tropical look. (Beware of notorious sandflies in this area.) As you approach the coast, listen as the sounds of tumbling waves grow louder and louder, and the nikau palms grow thicker. Suddenly, the empty beaches of the northwest coast come into view.

Beyond the sheer entertainment value of the shifting scenery, this trek is also notable for the opportunity to see some of New Zealand's unique wildlife, such as the kea, the planet's only alpine parrot, and great spotted kiwis, which call out to each other in the still of night. After dark, carnivorous land snails, which can grow to the size of baseballs, sneak out and slurp up three-foot-long (meter-long) worms. And if you're lucky, you might tick off a prized sighting of the takahe, a highly endangered flightless bird that was reintroduced in 2018. It is unmistakable with its beautiful, iridescent, blue-and-green back feathers.

ALTERNATIVE ROUTE

In late 2019, the Paparoa Track, a new "Great Walk" opened. Running 34 miles (55 km) through the Paparoa Range on the northwest side of the South Island, it offers hikers and mountain bikers access to rainforests, limestone karsts, and alpine zones with huts along the way. Views stretch across both the Tasman Sea and the Southern Alps.

THE KOKODA TRACK

The Ghosts of World War II

DISTANCE: 60 miles (96 km) one way   **LENGTH OF TRIP: 6 to 10 days**
BEST TIME TO GO: May through November   **DIFFICULTY: Strenuous**

During the second half of 1942, Japanese forces landed in Papua, intending to capture Port Moresby on the southern shore by traveling over the Owen Stanley Range. A vastly outnumbered group of Australian soldiers and Papuan allies waged a valiant defense. Part of a successful effort to stave off Japanese forces from commandeering key areas of the South Pacific, the Kokoda campaign is now renowned in the Australian history books. Today, the Kokoda Track loosely traces the routes soldiers used, and the trek has become a pilgrimage site for Australians seeking an immersion into a facet of their history—as well as a good old-fashioned challenge.

The elevation profile of this trek is like an EKG, beelining up steep, muddy mountainsides and back down only to charge straight across a river. Temperatures range from 75°F to 90°F (24–32°C) during the day and as low as the 30s (around 2°C) in high zones at night with a heaping dose of humidity. But the trip offers glimpses into the experiences of Australian soldiers as well as what daily life is like for Papuans, who have subsisted off the land, plants, and wildlife for centuries and often share their storytelling, singing, and dancing traditions with trekkers.

WHAT YOU'LL SEE: Historic war paths I Spotted cuscuses I Queen Alexandra's birdwing butterflies I Blue birds of paradise I Wild pigs

KNOW BEFORE YOU GO

The Kokoda Track Authority issues permits and licenses tour operators, who are strongly recommended to respect cultural customs and obtain permission to hike on private land. Go with a local service, if possible, and be culturally sensitive—dress modestly, don't bring alcohol, and don't disturb periods of worship in the evenings.

A hiker ascends the trail from a small village tucked away in the jungle.

DOVE LAKE CIRCUIT

Rainforests, Lakes, and Peaks

DISTANCE: 4.1 miles (6.6 km) round-trip   **LENGTH OF TRIP:** 2 to 3 hours
BEST TIME TO GO: Austral spring through fall   **DIFFICULTY:** Easy

In terms of reward for your effort, it's hard to beat the highly scenic Dove Lake Circuit, a mostly flat gravel-and-boardwalk loop through Tasmania's Cradle Mountain–Lake St. Clair National Park. Walking in a clockwise direction, hikers ramble through open buttongrass moorlands with low plants that allow views of the lake and the mountainous ridgelines that embrace it. As the path makes its way around the lake, you might stop on a sandy beach for a picnic or to take in the clarity of the water—and the trout that twist beneath the surface—or pause to observe a wallaby, a wombat, an echidna, or, if you're really lucky, a platypus. When the lake is still, it perfectly reflects the mountains and clouds above.

Boardwalks lead into ancient, mossy, temperate rainforests that this region of Tasmania is famed for. In these stands of myrtle-beech trees, draped with lichen, drink in the quiet sounds of birdsong and the breeze rushing over the land as you peer through the trunks to the primordial landscape of lake and peaks beyond. Perhaps the most photographed spot along the entire trail lies near the end: the Boatshed, a comely pine structure built in 1940 that still presides over the lake like a quiet sage.

WHAT YOU'LL SEE: Buttongrass moorlands | Trout | Wallabies | Wombats | Echidnas | Platypuses | Temperate rainforest | Myrtle-beech trees

THE CHALLENGE

The Overland Track is arguably Tasmania's most famous trek. It leads 38.8 miles (62.5 km) through the Tasmanian Wilderness World Heritage Area, from Cradle Mountain to Lake St. Clair, passing through open heathlands and moss-carpeted forests beneath the shadows of sheer cliffs, peaks, and waterfalls. A network of huts hosts hikers.

Cradle Mountain can be seen in the distance from the shoreline of Dove Lake.

THE LARAPINTA TRAIL

Australia's Red Desert Wilderness

DISTANCE: 139 miles (223 km) one way   **LENGTH OF TRIP:** 15 to 20 days
BEST TIME TO GO: Austral winter   **DIFFICULTY:** Moderate

For some 40,000 years, the Arrernte people have been living in the area around Alice Springs, way out in the Australian Outback. The land here is rich in cultural and spiritual significance and intricate origin stories. It is with permission from the indigenous people that visitors may now walk the Larapinta Trail, a long-distance path that traverses this ancestral territory—and a compelling journey through these wild desert expanses.

Visitors are often surprised that this desert is not simply a wasteland of sand but full of diverse sights and wonders. Check out the parade of red-rock formations, mountains, gorges, ridges, rare ponds, stands of trees, and greenery. Keep a keen eye out for black-footed rock wallabies and birds like kites, falcons, and adorable spinifex pigeons with their red, black, and white face patterns and striking head crest.

The Larapinta Trail is one of the newer long-distance trails in Australia, but already has a devoted following. People are attracted by the great expanses of land and sky, the wind, and the stillness that all invite a shift in perspective.

As you make your way west from Alice Springs, you'll walk across large plains with towering red rocks and stands of gum trees, then climb into the West MacDonnell Ranges. One memorable part of the first section is the

WILDLIFE SPOTTING

It's rare for hikers to see dingoes—wild dogs—but they do occasionally enter camps to maraud for human food. More likely, you will hear their howls. These canids live both alone and in packs and hunt for lizards, rodents, and birds. In parts of Australia, they are so numerous they are considered a nuisance.

OPPOSITE: After a heavy rain in the MacDonnell Ranges, the Ormiston Creek runs high.

NEXT PAGES: Seen from Hilltop Lookout, Mount Sonder glows red as the sun rises behind it.

tightrope-like walk across Razorback Ridge, a highly exposed backbone of rock with gigantic views.

"You have to slow down here. The rocks are really loose and everyone has to give everyone else a few meters of space," says Alice Homan, a guide for Australian Walking Holidays, a company that guides supported treks along the trail and runs a series of eco-camps for hikers. "But it's quite stunning—it feels like you can see to the edges of Australia."

After traversing the valley floor between ranges, hikers ascend back into the mountains. One welcome sight is Ellery Creek, a rare watering hole set in an embrace of rocky formations. Its serene water has inspired many weary hikers to take a frigid dip. Eventually, the trail ends at Mount Sonder, which rises 4,528 feet (1,380 m) above the desert and offers a spectacular view of the sunrise over this arid tableau.

KNOW BEFORE YOU GO

Be prepared for dramatic temperature fluctuations and high winds. Austral winter, between May and September, is the best time for walking, as temperatures float around 70°F (20°C or so) during the day. By contrast, in summer, the thermometer spikes as high as 120°F (nearly 50°C), and breezes feel like the exhaust from a dryer vent. Evening temperatures drop considerably in any season.

ABOVE: Palm-like cycads grow 6.5 feet (2 m) in width and length in the MacDonnell Ranges.

OPPOSITE: A rock wallaby and her joey pause for a moment as they climb the rocks of Rainbow Valley.

While the trail may not be very high, the challenges are numerous. Water is scarce and generally only available at trailheads, and the heat can feel punishing. While it's unlikely you'll encounter one, poisonous snakes, like the fearsome king brown, pose the biggest risk on the trail. But traveling through this harsh wilderness, which has held so much sacredness for human beings for so many millennia, is also profoundly moving. Consider some of the quietest moments on the trail—drinking in the fresh, earthy scent of the land after precious rain, listening to the eerie howls of dingoes after dark, or watching mist lift off the rocks mysteriously.

"You really have that isolation feeling, which is a big calling point for people," says Homan. "It's hard to imagine how big the land is out there . . . You'll be standing up on a high point and the horizon just sort of disappears—it just goes and goes and goes."

BIBBULMUN TRACK

The Lands of the Nyoongar

DISTANCE: About 620 miles (1,000 km) one way
BEST TIME TO GO: Austral fall, winter, and spring
LENGTH OF TRIP: 6 to 8 weeks
DIFFICULTY: Moderate

The Nyoongar people have lived in the southwest region of western Australia for some 45,000 years, holding profound connections to the land. One group of the Nyoongar, the Bibbulmun, lived in the forests around Pemberton and, like other indigenous people in the region, took long walks for ceremonial purposes. When hiking enthusiasts hatched the idea for a long-distance trail in the region in the 1970s, Bibbulmun seemed a fitting name to honor those who lived on and cared for the land for so many centuries.

After many iterations and reroutings, the Bibbulmun Track now extends about 620 miles (1,000 km) from Kalamunda, a suburb outside of Perth, to Albany along the very southwestern knob of the Australian continent. Seven towns and 49 established campsites, which feature shelters and rainwater tanks, dot the route, making it an appealing foray into long-distance trekking for those who may not have a lot of deep wilderness experience.

The vast majority of hikers on the Bibbulmun Track bite off daylong or short multiday chunks, but every year, about 120 people, known as "end-to-enders," tackle the entire thing. The majority start in the north in spring and hike south into colder zones as the landscape heats up. One of the great joys of this track is the wide diversity of plant life—the southwestern chunk of western Australia is known for its biodiversity and endemic species.

ALTERNATIVE ROUTE

One of the most diverse shorter sections of the trail leads 78 miles (126 km) between Walpole and Denmark, hitting forests of karri and tingle trees, including the aptly named Valley of the Giants, the community of Peaceful Bay, and coastal stretches with steep sand dunes, heaths, and empty beaches.

OPPOSITE: The Tree Top Walk bridge spans the canopy of the Valley of the Giants inside Walpole-Nornalup National Park.

NEXT PAGES: A western rosella perches in the bushes.

WHAT YOU'LL SEE: Jarrah forests I Karri trees I
Wildflowers I Tingle trees I Beaches I Sand dunes I
Cliffs I Bays I Dugite and tiger snakes I Goannas I
Skinks I Wedgetail eagles I Emus I Cockatoos

For the first half of the trail, the loose jarrah forests predominate. Hikers travel through the Darling Range, where they'll climb up knobs and peaks like Mount Cooke for views of the landscape. Keep an eye out for the unusual butter gum tree as you pass through these open woodlands. In the Murray River Valley, serene pools beckon to weary trekkers for a dip.

At about the halfway mark, the vegetation changes completely and gigantic karri trees, the world's third tallest trees, take over. In spring, wildflowers shoot up out of the earth, painting the forest floor in drops of purple, orange, and yellow. In this forest of giants, you will also commune with the tingle trees, which are massive in girth as opposed to height—some 20 people can link arms and still not make it around the base of one of these behemoths. Finally, the scent of the sea floats through the air and grows stronger as

KNOW BEFORE YOU GO

The Bibbulmun Track Foundation, which supports trail maintenance and informs hikers, works hard to deter trekkers from attempting the trail in the summertime. Bush fires are a major hazard and some hikers have nearly perished in them. In January 2018, a hiker was plucked by a helicopter from a campsite, which was consumed by wildfire within 10 minutes of the rescue.

ABOVE: **A winding stairway leads to secluded Salmon Holes beach—an excellent fishing spot—in Torndirrup National Park.**

OPPOSITE: **Colorful West Australian wildflowers, like the coral vine, grow along the track's route.**

hikers approach the coast. As the trail meanders along the shore, it reveals a world of untamed beaches, huge crescent-shaped bays, sand dunes, and cliffs. From the top of granite outcroppings, one can gaze across the landscape of forest and sea.

Hikers often see wildlife on the quieter sections of the Bibbulmun Track. Be aware of the highly venomous (but shy and fearful) dugite and tiger snake, both of which are commonly seen. You might also see goannas and skinks sunning themselves on rocks, and birds, like the magnificent wedge-tail eagle, the elusive emu, the colorful rosella, or cockatoos, high in the treetops. Nighttime is when the marsupials, such as echidnas or quendas, emerge. In the quiet of darkness, listen for their sounds—like the thump of a kangaroo hop—and wake up to the presence of the other little critters that inhabit this wonderland, like a tiny tree frog eyeing you from outside your mosquito net.

THE SHACKLETON HIKE

A Great Explorer's Route

DISTANCE: About 4 miles (6 km) one way   **LENGTH OF TRIP:** 3 to 4 hours
BEST TIME TO GO: Austral summer   **DIFFICULTY:** Moderate

Situated way out in the southern Atlantic Ocean, about 1,300 miles (2,100 km) east of Tierra del Fuego in Argentina, South Georgia Island is a brooding enclave of charcoal mountains, glaciers, and rocky shores. Essentially a chunk of the Andes that drifted out to sea some 50 million years ago, this island is so big and formidable it creates its own weather patterns. To call the conditions hostile would be an understatement: In summer, it's not uncommon for temperatures to stay in the 20s Fahrenheit (below zero Celsius) and for fierce winds to crop up at a moment's notice.

This is where Ernest Shackleton, the famed early 20th-century Antarctic explorer, found himself after a Hail Mary bid to rescue his expedition crew. The men had already spent more than a year traveling across ice and sea after their ship had been crushed in the pack ice. They were marooned on Elephant Island when Shackleton and five of his men sailed 800 miles (nearly 1,300 km) across frigid, stormy seas, navigating by sextant, to seek help on South Georgia, the only mote of civilization in hundreds of square miles of sea.

But after landing, the team still had one last tribulation: They had to traverse the spiny, ice-clad island on foot to a whaling station. Shackleton and his two strongest men completed the hair-raising 26-mile (42-km) route in a mere

HISTORICAL FOOTNOTE

Despite the trials of his previous experience in the Antarctic, Ernest Shackleton couldn't seem to pull himself away from the lure of the pole. In 1922, on another expedition, he died of a heart attack aboard his ship moored near the whaling station of Grytviken. He was buried in its cemetery, his grave facing south.

OPPOSITE: Hikers set out along the Shackleton Hike from Fortuna Bay to Stromness.
NEXT PAGES: Ship propellers lie among resting Antarctic fur seals at a historic whaling station on the northern coast of South Georgia Island.

WHAT YOU'LL SEE: King penguins I Fur seals I
Elephant seals I Albatross I Crean Lake I
Historic whaling station

36 hours, a feat that modern mountaineers still consider mind-blowing under the circumstances. Needless to say, the workers at the whaling station were very surprised to see them. Eventually, they launched a rescue mission to Elephant Island and all of Shackleton's men survived the ordeal. The episode is still legendary in the annals of exploration history and has become an oft-told parable for those learning leadership and perseverance.

Nowadays, South Georgia Island is still one of the world's great wildernesses. Few tourists come here, and there is only one way: by ship. It takes many days of open ocean travel, often in seas with big swells and high winds. For long stretches, there is nothing on the horizon but water. For those who do venture here, retracing the steps of one of the greatest rescue stories of all time is a hallowed rite. The entire route is generally only tackled by mountaineers, but the last stretch,

WILDLIFE SPOTTING

The cold seas around South Georgia contain feasts of fish and krill for marine creatures and birds. Discover colonies of up to 100,000 king penguins, emitting a cacophony of kazoo-like calls. Walk among fur seal pups—watch out for their fierce mamas, which sometimes bluff-charge—and elephant seals as big as cars. The gargantuan wandering albatross also nests here.

ABOVE: Antarctic fur seal pups play on the ice on the beach at Fortuna Bay.

OPPOSITE: Ernest Shackleton's grave lies in the Grytviken Cemetery on South Georgia Island.

between Fortuna Bay and Stromness, is a reasonable chunk for hikers to bite off in a day.

Upon landing at Fortuna Bay, you'll likely be greeted by a welcome party of penguins, who, with no land predators, are endearingly fearless and friendly. Fur seals dot the shore, lounge in the tussocks, and galumph to and fro. Myriad birds soar overhead. Climb up the grassy hills and loose, rocky mountainsides, passing by Crean Lake and a couple of small tarns before reaching a pass at about 1,000 feet (300 m), then descend to a point where you can see the remnants of the whaling station below. This is where Shackleton heard the whistle of the station and knew he was, after a Herculean effort, within reach of help. As you pick your way down through the slope of loose stones and through a flat valley to the shore, imagine what it must have felt like to finally see other human beings after some two years stuck in one of the coldest, harshest places on Earth.

THE LAVENA COASTAL WALK

Beaches, Jungles, and Waterfalls

DISTANCE: About 6 miles (10 km) round-trip   **LENGTH OF TRIP:** 2 to 4 hours
BEST TIME TO GO: Year-round   **DIFFICULTY:** Moderate

In the early 1990s, on the Fijian island of Taveuni, four villages of the Bouma tribe founded Bouma National Heritage Park and developed tourist attractions in an effort to establish sustainable livelihoods. One of the results was the Lavena Coastal Walk, a trail that starts from the eponymous village and leads along light-sand beaches, fringed with lush rainforest on one side and turquoise lagoons on the other.

The trail wends near small settlements where local children might shyly eye visitors, wave, or even come out and return a high five and a smile. There are a few easy river crossings as you make your way along the trail. Eventually, the beaches turn to black sand and volcanic stone, and the route nosedives into the jungle, following a rocky riverbed.

Fiji is known for an abundance of unique species—keep a careful eye out for the Taveuni silktail, an endemic bird that has rich, velvety, blue-and-black plumage. Giant ferns and forest trees cram the edges of the waterway as you pick your way up to a wonderful treat: Wainibau Falls. To see it in its full glory, you must swim up a small dark gorge cloaked in vibrant emerald plants to an alcove where you're immersed in the spray and sounds of rushing water.

WHAT YOU'LL SEE: Waterfalls I Black-sand and volcanic stone beaches I Rainforest I Lagoons I Taveuni silktails I Giant ferns

CULTURAL IMMERSION

Kava, also known as *yaqona*, is the beverage of choice for Fijians, who imbibe it together in kava ceremonies. Made from a root found in the region, the drink, which tastes earthy and slightly bitter, does not contain any alcohol but produces a mild and relaxing sense of euphoria.

The Lavena Coastal Walk crosses through verdant jungle landscapes and sandy beach alcoves.

THE ROUTEBURN TRACK

The Great Southern Alps

DISTANCE: 20.5 miles (33 km) one way   **LENGTH OF TRIP:** 2 to 4 days
BEST TIME TO GO: Austral summer   **DIFFICULTY:** Moderate

The territory between Fiordland National Park and Mount Aspiring National Park on New Zealand's South Island was once the domain of powerful glaciers. Everywhere you look, the results of their artistry remain: plunging fjords, tarns, and angular ridges. The Routeburn Track is not New Zealand's most difficult or longest trek, but it offers a brief, powerful introduction to the country's legendary alpine terrain.

Hikers ("trampers," as the locals would say) typically take three days to travel the path one way. Four huts punctuate the trail and, during the summer months, offer gas stoves for cooking, bunks, a resident ranger who can answer questions, and a lively atmosphere of international travelers. (Make reservations ahead of time—and earplugs aren't a bad idea.) The vast majority of hikers tackle this trek in the Southern Hemisphere's summer, between mid-October and April. In winter, rangers take most of the bridges down so that they don't get pulverized by avalanches and floods, which means that hikers who attempt the trek must be highly skilled in winter backcountry travel.

While storms can roll in any month of the year and bring rain and wind, walking in summer is often positively delightful. This is one of New Zealand's so-called "Great Walks," which means it is particularly well-maintained, wider than many other single-track routes, and relatively easy to walk. The scenery is so consistently spectacular that some hikers have described it as walking

OPPOSITE: After hiking, hop on a jet boat to speed along the Shotover River just outside of Queenstown.

NEXT PAGES: As you make your way through Fiordland National Park along the track, take in majestic views of snowcapped peaks reflected in alpine lakes.

through a postcard. Amble silently through forests lined with a sea of fluffy ferns. Feel puny as you gaze up at steep, dark mountainsides from a grassy valley floor. Ogle giant waterfalls that cascade down rocky slabs, and watch as the mists come and go, making the landscape feel ancient and fairy-tale-like.

The highest point is Harris Saddle, also known as Tarahaka Whakatipu, at 4,117 feet (1,255 m). If the fog disperses, a vista of raggedy peaks unfolds in all directions. Lower down, take an icy dip in an alpine lake or in the pool of a waterfall. Keep on the lookout for rare birds like the blue duck, or *whio,* and the rock wren, or *tuke.* And take time to be still; some of the most beautiful moments might arise while you're not actually moving. Outside of Lake Mackenzie Hut, bask on the shores of the eponymous lake as the light ebbs from the sky and the glassy surface of the pond reflects the mountains and sky above.

POST-HIKE ACTIVITY

Not far from the start of the Routeburn Track, Queenstown is the famed adventure hub of New Zealand's Southern Alps. In summer, try whitewater rafting, skydiving, and bungee jumping in the sport's birthplace. Winter brings skiing, and the nearby Central Otago wine region is known for its Pinot Noirs.

OBSERVATION HILL, MCMURDO STATION

Antarctica's After-Work Hike

DISTANCE: 0.8 miles (1.3 km) round-trip   **LENGTH OF TRIP:** 1 to 2 hours
BEST TIME TO GO: Austral summer   **DIFFICULTY:** Moderate

A dark-rock lava dome striking up out of the vast Antarctic white, Observation Hill is essentially the after-work hike for researchers and workers assigned to McMurdo Station, a hub for the U.S. Antarctic Program. Located at the end of a peninsula on Ross Island, the settlement consists of airstrips, a harbor, and about 85 buildings. As many as 950 people reside here during the austral summer when temperatures hover in the relatively balmy 20s and low 30s Fahrenheit (–11 to –4 Celsius).

It's not easy to get here—you must have a research grant, a work contract with one of the contractors that supports the station, or perhaps you're launching an expedition. But, chances are, if you arrive in the summer, when the midnight sun circles the sky, you will want to climb to the top of this upstanding mound for a look at your surroundings. Navigation is virtually nil—you can't miss the hill on a sunny day. Simply walk through the crushed-rock roads of McMurdo Station and follow the stone-and-snow trail that leads to the top of this 750-foot (228-m) hill. The summit affords views over the immense monochrome of the ice shelves; the Transantarctic Mountains; Mount Discovery and Mount Erebus, an active volcano; and McMurdo station and New Zealand's Scott Base below.

WHAT YOU'LL SEE: McMurdo Station | Ice shelves | Transantarctic Mountains

HISTORICAL FOOTNOTE

In 1912, Robert Falcon Scott and a team of explorers perished on their way back from an attempt to reach the South Pole first. (They arrived to find that Norwegian Roald Amundsen had beat them to it.) On Ob Hill, a memorial wooden cross now bears their names and words from Tennyson: "To strive, to seek, to find, and not to yield."

Observation Hill looks out over the McMurdo Station research buildings, Mount Erebus, the Transantarctic Mountains, and Mount Discovery.

HIKING CONSERVATION

As hikers, we have the good fortune of seeing the world's most magnificent corners. Majestic mountain peaks, dormant volcanoes, highland meadows, desert dunes, and lush marshlands are our oasis—the scenes and wonders that draw us back to the trail time and time again. It is our responsibility to protect and preserve these wild places and the wildlife that lives within them before they're lost forever.

Hikers should be leading the charge to protect our wilderness areas because we are in the privileged position to see the changes taking place firsthand. It's our backyard and our responsibility.

Not sure where to begin? Here are eight conservation guidelines to get you started:

1. **Vote.** This is an easy—and important—one. Vote for politicians who champion conservation and let them (and their opponents) know why. Be vocal. Sign petitions. For as much good as we're doing individually, we need lawmakers to back it up on a global level.

2. **Support science.** Misinformation and choked-off funding are making scientific research difficult, right when we need it most. Whether it's a local grassroots project in your community, organizations looking at the larger picture, or solution-focused companies, you can provide support by donating your time, volunteering your individual expertise (be it graphic design or social media know-how), or backing these organizations financially. Hikers should also consider becoming citizen scientists by monitoring and documenting your surroundings on hikes and making note of climate conditions.

3. **Drive less.** Get to your next trailhead via carpool or public transportation. According to the EPA, America's transportation sector was responsible for 26 percent of green-

house gas emissions in 2014. Ride public buses where you can, carpool when you can't, and use websites and apps to find car-free options to reach outdoor destinations.

4. **Look but don't touch.** This should be a no-brainer, but in the age of Instagram, we could all use another reminder: Let wildlife choose the interaction. Give animals space, and *never* touch or feed animals. Avoid (and report) any operation that doesn't apply good practice or alters the behavior of wildlife.

5. **Plant trees.** Instead of muddying up those boots, get a little dirt on your hands. Plants help absorb carbon dioxide from the atmosphere and offset carbon emissions. In 2014, the EPA reported the land use and forestry sector offset 11 percent of greenhouse gas emissions. Plant your own trees, or donate to organizations that do the work for you.

6. **Volunteer.** Hiking trails don't maintain themselves. Help preserve the routes you love the most by volunteering as a trail steward. Bring friends—of any age—to help clean debris, mark routes, restore plants, and more. Come June, participate in the American Hiking Society's National Trails Day to give back to the places you love to explore the most.

7. **Support the parks.** Donate. Volunteer. Supporting our national parks, forests, waterways, nature reserves, and more help keep the wilderness places safe.

8. **Remember that plastic is not so fantastic.** In May 2018 National Geographic launched its Planet or Plastic? campaign, a multiyear effort to raise awareness about the global plastic crisis. A few fast plastic facts for you:
    - More than 40 percent of plastic is used once and then discarded, and 6.3 billion tons (5.7 billion metric tons) of plastic fill our landfills, landscapes, and oceans.
    - Nearly one million plastic bottles are sold every minute around the world.
    - Plastic takes nearly 400 years to degrade; a 2018 study found that only 9 percent of plastics are recycled.

Be mindful of the amount of plastic you use in your everyday life and take active steps to reduce it. You can do this while hiking and backpacking by bringing reusable water bottles with you, as well as multiuse utensils that you can pull out instead of the plastic stuff. Oh, and skip the plastic straws, please. It's that simple. And that effective.

DESTINATIONS BY LOCATION

ACKNOWLEDGMENTS

Almost all the trails in this book wind through publicly owned land. They exist because countless people pioneered, built, and maintained them. I'd like to thank all the dedicated park rangers, land managers, conservationists, trail builders, scientists, volunteers, and other trail lovers whose hard work protects these lands and trails for our own enjoyment and for the benefit of our children and future generations.

A book never comes into being through the efforts of just one person, and *100 Hikes of a Lifetime* is no exception. In addition to my own experience hiking many of these areas, I relied on the generosity and expertise of numerous experts and guides, from Andrew Skurka, the long-distance hiker and National Geographic adventurer, to the warm, welcoming, and skilled guides and travelers I have met through the Adventure Travel Trade Association. Thank you for sharing your wonderful expertise from all corners of the globe.

I'd also like to thank the hikers, park employees, guides, and tourism staffers who generously gave me hours of their time to confirm details about these walks that might have faded from my memory over time. Your knowledge and willingness to share has improved this book immeasurably. I have deep admiration and appreciation for the team at National Geographic, including Allyson Johnson, Krista Rossow, Judith Klein, and Nicole Miller. Thank you for helping the process of creating *100 Hikes* unfold so seamlessly and beautifully.

I have also enjoyed much support in the activity of hiking itself. While I occasionally travel solo, hiking wouldn't be the same without some of my favorite partners in adventure. Thank you Andrew, Ryan, Anna, Eileen, Amy, Kara, Ellen, Rachel, Amanda, Lori, Diana, and so many others for joining me on jaunts into the natural world both near and far, and for your friendship.

ABOUT THE AUTHOR

KATE SIBER is a freelance journalist and a correspondent for *Outside* magazine. Her work has appeared in *National Geographic Traveler, National Parks, 5280,* the *Boston Globe,* the *New York Times,* and the *Washington Post,* among many other newspapers and magazines, and has been honored with several Lowell Thomas awards, including Travel Journalist of the Year. In 2018, her children's book, *National Parks of the U.S.A.,* a large-format, illustrated tour of the country's great parks for kids ages six to nine, was published by Wide Eyed Editions.

When she is not writing or reading, Kate Siber is generally outside—hiking, backpacking, running, skiing, swimming, paddleboarding, diving, meditating, staring at clouds, collecting mushrooms, and wandering the wilderness wherever she can find it. She grew up hiking in New England, but one of her all-time favorite places to explore on foot is the Grand Canyon, where the geological record offers an incomparable sense of perspective.

Find Kate Siber on Instagram (@sibereye), on Twitter (@katesiber), or at her website, katesiber.com.

ANDREW SKURKA (foreword) is an accomplished adventure athlete, speaker, guide, and writer. He has been named Adventurer of the Year by *Outside* magazine and National Geographic, and Person of the Year by *Backpacker* magazine. He is the author of *The Ultimate Hiker's Gear Guide,* now in its second edition. Skurka is most well known for his solo long-distance hiking trips. He has pioneered four off-trail backpacking routes and has created guidebooks for each and leads learning-intensive backpacking trips. When not living out of his backpack, he resides with his wife in Boulder, Colorado.

ILLUSTRATIONS CREDITS

Cover, Elliot Hawkey; Back cover, StevanZZ/Alamy Stock Photo; 1, ImpossiAble/Getty Images; 2-3, Tomas Zrna/Getty Images; 4-5, Krista Rossow; 7, Andrew Coleman/National Geographic Image Collection; 8, George Ostertag/Alamy Stock Photo; 11, Udi Goren; 14-15, Michele Falzone/Getty Images; 17, Christopher Kimmel/Getty Images; 18-19, Rich Wheater/All Canada Photos/Alamy Stock Photo; 21, John Elk III/Getty Images; 22-3, Susan Seubert; 25, Christian Goupi/age fotostock/Alamy Stock Photo; 27, Noppawat Tom Charoensinphon/Getty Images; 28-9, Adria Photography/Getty Images; 30, Michael Melford/Getty Images; 31, Scott Dickerson/Design Pics Inc/National Geographic Image Collection; 33, Carolyn Brown/Getty Images; 34-5, Arturo Peña Romano Med/Getty Images; 37, HagePhoto/Cavan Images; 38-9, Greg Jaggears/Getty Images; 40, Corey Rich/Cavan Images; 41, HagePhoto/Cavan Images; 43, Eric Guth; 44-5, Anna Mazurek; 47, Rob Hammer/Cavan Images; 48-9, Francesco Riccardo Iacomino/AWL Images/Cavan Images; 50, Cavan Images/Getty Images; 51, Gemina Garland-Lewis; 53, Jose Azel/Getty Images; 54-5, Jose Azel/Getty Images; 56, Deemwave/Shutterstock; 57, Travel Images/UIG/Getty Images; 59, Hannah Dewey/Getty Images; 60-61, Lee Rentz/Alamy Stock Photo; 63, Kevin Boutwell/Getty Images; 64-5, Piriya Photography/Getty Images; 67, Malcolm MacGregor/Getty Images; 68-9, Michael D. Wilson/Cavan Images; 71, Jad Davenport/National Geographic Image Collection; 72-3, Rachid Dahnoun; 75, Ralph Lee Hopkins/National Geographic Image Collection; 76-7, Bennett Barthelemy/TandemStock.com; 79, Stanley Chen Xi/Getty Images; 81, Braian mac/Shutterstock; 83, Frans Lanting/lanting.com; 84-5, Daniela Linares/Anzenberger/Redux; 87, Ben Herndon/TandemStock.com; 88-9, Paul Tessier/Shutterstock; 90-91, Erika Skogg; 93, Rodrigo S. Coelho/Shutterstock.com; 94-5, Creative Family/Shutterstock.com; 96, Ben Pipe/robertharding/National Geographic Image Collection; 97, flocu/Shutterstock; 99, Fabio Liverani/NPL/Minden Pictures; 100-1, Lucas Bustamante/NPL/Minden Pictures; 103, Ketkarn Sakultap/Getty Images; 104-105, Blaine Harrington III/Getty Images; 106, McPHOTO/age fotostock; 107, Tolo Balaguer/age fotostock; 109, Colin Harris/era-images/Alamy Stock Photo; 110-11, Courtesy of Cascada Expediciones; 113, Lucas Vallecillos/Alamy Stock Photo; 114-15, Ignacio Palacios/Getty Images; 117, Last Refuge/robertharding/Getty Images; 119, Romulo Rejon/Getty Images; 121, Bart Heirweg/Buiten-beeld/Minden Pictures; 122-3, Christian Kober/robertharding/Getty Images; 125, Philippe Henry/Getty Images; 126-7, Glenn Oakley/Cavan Images; 129, Peek Creative Collective/Alamy Stock Photo; 130-31, Daniel Noll, Uncornered Market; 133, gorilonpictures/Shutterstock; 135, Alex Treadway/National Geographic Image Collection; 137, Max Shen/Getty Images; 138-9, Alex Treadway/National Geographic Image Collection; 141, Açony Santos; 143, Mauricio Handler/National Geographic Image Collection; 144-5, Mauricio Handler/National Geographic Image Collection; 146-7, PatitucciPhoto; 149, Matthew Karsten; 150-51, Matthew Karsten; 152, Matthew Karsten; 153, Martin Zwick/Danita Delimont/Getty Images; 155, Revirado/Alamy Stock Photo; 156-7, Franck Guiziou/hemis.fr/Getty Images; 159, Lookphotos /Jürgen Richter/Cavan Images; 160-61, Jim Richardson/National Geographic Image Collection; 162, Reinhard Schmid/Huber Images/eStock Photo; 163, Juergen Richter/LOOK-foto/Getty Images; 165, Gareth McCormack/Getty Images; 167, Westend61/Martin Rietze/Getty Images; 168-9, Robbie Shone/National Geographic Image Collection; 171, StevanZZ/Alamy Stock Photo; 173, ClickAlps/mauritius images GmbH/Alamy Stock Photo; 174-5, PatitucciPhoto; 176, Achim Thomae/Getty Images; 177, Eddie Gianelloni Media/Cavan Images; 179, Alan Wilson/Alamy Stock Photo; 180-81, Menno Boermans/Cavan Images; 183, Menno Boermans/Cavan Images; 185, Raffi Maghdessian/Getty Images; 187, Kreuels/laif/Redux;

188-9, Matteo Colombo/Getty Images; 190, ollo/Getty Images; 191, Johann Scheibner/imageBROKER/Alamy Stock Photo; 193, Mario Weigt/Anzenberger/Redux; 194-5, Mario Weigt/Anzenberger/Redux; 197, Cole Rise; 198-9, visitnorway.com/Sverre Hjørnevik; 201, Christopher Simpson/Gallery Stock; 203, Erlend Haarberg/National Geographic Image Collection; 204-205, Orsolya Haarberg/National Geographic Image Collection; 207, Quentin Penn-Hollar; 209, Chris Hill/National Geographic Image Collection; 210-11, Chris Hill/National Geographic Image Collection; 212, Dave Yoder/National Geographic Image Collection; 213, Henglein and Steets/Cultura/Cavan Images; 215, Jing Shi; 217, christographerowens/Shutterstock; 219, James Osmond/Alamy Stock Photo; 220-21, Matthew Williams-Ellis/robertharding/National Geographic Image Collection; 222, Martin Siepmann/imageBROKER/Alamy Stock Photo; 223, Markus Kirchgessner/laif/Redux; 225, Andrea Pozzi/Getty Images; 226-7, lifght_reader/Alamy Stock Photo; 228, Adnan Bubalo; 229, Julien Garcia/Getty Images; 231, Natasa Kirin/Alamy Stock Photo; 233, Franz Gerdl/Carinthian Tourism Board; 234-5, Horst-Dieter Zinn/laif/Redux; 236-7, Beverly Joubert/National Geographic Image Collection; 239, Frits Meyst/MeystPhoto.com; 240-41, Frits Meyst/MeystPhoto.com; 242, David Degner; 243, Frits Meyst/MeystPhoto.com; 245, Dani Stein; 247, Markus Mauthe/laif/Redux; 248-9, Visuals Unlimited, Inc./Robert Pickett/Getty Images; 251, Christian Heeb/laif/Redux; 253, Jørn Eriksson/Getty Images; 254-5, Martin Zwick/DanitaDelimont/Getty Images; 256, Nobuo Matsumura/Alamy Stock Photo; 257, Ronan Donovan/National Geographic Image Collection; 259, Visionsof America.com/Joe Sohm/Getty Images; 261, Herman du Plessis/Getty Images; 263, David Pluth/National Geographic Image Collection; 264-5, George Robertson/Getty Images; 267, Chantal de Bruijne/Shutterstock; 268-9, picture alliance/Getty Images; 271, Peter Langer/DanitaDelimont/Alamy Stock Photo; 273, Ronan Donovan/National Geographic Image Collection; 274-5, Ronan Donovan/National Geographic Image Collection; 277, Nick Garbutt/Barcroft Media/Getty Images; 279, Yury Birukov/Shutterstock; 280-81, Michael Runkel/robertharding/National Geographic Image Collection; 282, Jason Gallier/Alamy Stock Photo; 283, Roy Schwarz/DanitaDelimont/Alamy Stock Photo; 285, Michael Poliza/National Geographic Image Collection; 287, Emil von Maltitz/Getty Images; 289, Eric Nathan/Alamy Stock Photo; 290-91, Khanthachai C/Shutterstock; 293, Nick Brundle Photography/Getty Images; 294-5, Udi Goren; 296, Udi Goren; 297, Udi Goren; 299, Aloïs Peiffer/Getty Images; 301, Martin Stolworthy/Design Pics Inc/National Geographic Image Collection; 302-303, traumlichtfabrik/Getty Images; 304, Constantin Stanciu/Shutterstock.com; 305, Jamie McGuinness—Project Himalaya/Getty Images; 307, Stephen Lioy; 309, FEBRUARY/Getty Images; 310-11, Manish Lakhani/Alamy Stock Photo; 313, Fiona Li/EyeEm/Getty Images; 314-15, Thanwan Singh Pannu/Getty Images; 317, Michele Falzone/Alamy Stock Photo; 319, Traveller. P/Shutterstock; 320-21, Pascal Boegli/Getty Images; 323, happystock/Shutterstock; 325, Peter Stuckings/Getty Images; 326-7, Alan Copson/robertharding/National Geographic Image Collection; 329, Suttipong Sutiratanachai/Getty Images; 331, Neale Cousland/Shutterstock; 332-3, Liyao Xie/Getty Images; 335, Ethan Welty/Cavan Images; 336-7, Anastasios71/Shutterstock; 339, Dmitry Rukhlenko—Travel Photos/Alamy Stock Photo; 341, Michael Mellinger/Getty Images; 343, Aaron Huey/National Geographic Image Collection; 345, Suphanat Wongsanuphat/Getty Images; 346-7, Manish Lakhani/Alamy Stock Photo; 348, Cavan Images/Getty Images; 349, Ben Pipe/robertharding/Alamy Stock Photo; 351, Alongkot Sumritjearapol/Getty Images; 353, Sayid Budhi/Getty Images; 354-5, Nick Groves/Hedgehog House/Minden Pictures/National Geographic Image Collection; 357, new zealand transition/Getty Images; 358-9, Shaun Barnett/Hedgehog House/Minden Pictures/National Geographic Image Collection; 361, Andrew Peacock/Getty Images; 363, Rebecca North/500px/Getty Images; 365, Ingo Oeland/Alamy Stock Photo; 366-7, Posnov/Getty Images; 368, Nolan Caldwell/Getty Images; 369, Posnov/Getty Images; 371, Kevin Schafer/Alamy Stock Photo; 372-3, Alex Courtier/Alamy Stock Photo; 374, Suzanne Long/Alamy Stock Photo; 375, Andrew Watson/Getty Images; 377, Jeff Mauritzen; 378-9, Ralph Lee Hopkins/National Geographic Image Collection; 380, Alexey Seafarer/Shutterstock.com; 381, Michael Nolan/robertharding/National Geographic Image Collection; 383, Don Mammoser/Shutterstock; 385, Krista Rossow; 386-7, Colin Monteath/Hedgehog House/Minden Pictures/National Geographic Image Collection; 389, Alasdair Turner/Cavan Images.

Since 1888, the National Geographic Society has funded more than 13,000 research, exploration, and preservation projects around the world. National Geographic Partners distributes a portion of the funds it receives from your purchase to National Geographic Society to support programs including the conservation of animals and their habitats.

National Geographic Partners
1145 17th Street NW
Washington, DC 20036-4688 USA

Get closer to National Geographic explorers and photographers, and connect with our global community. Join us today at nationalgeographic.com/join.

For rights or permissions inquiries, please contact National Geographic Books Subsidiary Rights: bookrights@natgeo.com

ISBN: 978-1-4262-2095-1

Printed in the United States of America

20/VP-PCML/2

The information in this book has been carefully checked and to the best of our knowledge is accurate. However, details are subject to change, and the publisher cannot be responsible for such changes, or for errors or omissions. Assessments of sites, hotels, and restaurants are based on the author's subjective opinions, which do not necessarily reflect the publisher's opinion.